P9-BZX-176

MY EYES HAVE SEEN

The
Autobiography
of

Louis Lazarus Trenton

Toronto 2008

© 2008 Louis Trenton

All rights reserved. No part of this publication may be reproduced, stored in retrieval system, or transmitted, in any form or by any means, electronic, mechanical, photocopying, recording or otherwise, without the prior written permission of the author.

ISBN 978-0-9809656-1-2

Cover and layout design by Ekaterina Todorova

National Library of Canada

Contact information:
Lou Trenton
25 SHIELDS AVE. TORONTO
ONTARIO CANADA M5N 2K1
Or E mail:
lltrenton@sympatico.ca

One does not choose when one's life begins, one's parents or many of the events in one's formative years. However at a given point in all of our lives, we begin to make decisions and choose our paths.

The story that appears on the following pages is a summary of the choices that were made for me and by me, as well as the luck, misfortune and opportunities I have experienced in my life.

My hope is that my story will be read by present and future generations of my family. After all, one's roots are a guide: If you don't know where you have come from, you don't know where you are going.

This publication would not have been created without the advice and guidance of my editor and loving daughter, Becky Nenka Trenton Norman

CONTENTS

Chapter 1

BORN: ZHELEVO / ANTARTIKON

The snow was gently drifting on a remote village nestled in the mountains of northern Greece in the province of Macedonia where I drew my first breath.

The tale my dear mother, Nenka, related to me was that I was still-born, or so she thought. It was only with the aid of a midwife's large hand across my rump that I was forced to inhale. It was in the wee hours of the morning as the dawn was slowly appearing. My mother remarked that I had a large, light head and the appearance of an albino. She said I resembled an angel.

During that period in time my father was labouring in America (Toronto, Canada) trying to earn a living and save money for transportation to migrate our family of four, which included my mother, sister, brother and I. This was no small task for a man with no trade or talent for earning a living in a strange country and with a great disability; he could not speak the English language and was a stranger to the customs of his new adopted country. He only had a strong desire to adapt to the Canadian culture and succeed.

My mother claims that, as an infant, I was always hungry. I would eat any food that was presented to me. It was a time of no electricity in the homes and streets of the small towns in that corner of the world. In the winter months, we all huddled in one large room, with a fireplace which was also utilized for cooking. We would dine and then sleep on mats on the dry mud floor. This same space served as all-purpose room. In the evenings it was our entertainment room for swapping tales of the day and expounding our fiction and factual stories.

My mother did her share of labour on the farm. Some days, I was transported papoose-style (similar to the North American Indians) in a pouch worn by the women in those days. I was strapped on her back, facing outwards with my face exposed to the bright sun, wind and flies. Not able to speak or protest at that tender age, mothers were not aware of what had to be endured by the child.

The other normal procedure was wrapping the babies in a heavy thick blanket with its little arms and legs in a straight position, bound by a thick yellow rope. If I had been able to communicate, I would have yelled, "It's too tight Ma, it's too tight."

All infants, at that stage in life, have no way of expressing themselves so they cry. That's normal and taken for granted and ignored. Therefore, the torture prevailed and was endured by the baby.

A male never helped nurture or carried the baby papoose-style. It was not the manly thing to do. So, most of my infant days were spent being carried by the women designated to clean and prepare the noon repast for the family labouring in the fields. Some days, I would be left behind to sleep. Other times I would be carried papoose-style, freeing the woman's arms to carry the lunch.

Lunch consisted of a wooden pail with beans or stew and feta cheese or olives and bread that was wrapped in a cloth. This meal was carried out to the field a distance away. A lonely, sad donkey was utilized for all duties including transporting the food, if the donkey was not needed for heavier choirs in the field.

Arriving with the lunch, the first face I would often see was my dear mother's, attempting to unload the food off the back of that stubborn donkey. A monumental task at times. The donkey was an unpredictable, cantankerous creature that would instantly, and without notice, throw a tantrum for no reason at all. Our donkey did not like me very much and the feeling was mutual.

My sweet mother unloaded my small carcass from the back of the person carrying me; to the relief of the woman and to the great joy to my mother. We lunched together. She masticated the food and placed portion of it in my mouth. The rest of my family satisfied their hunger then all came around "goo" and "gaa" over me.

After lunch they all headed back to their respective duty to labour in the fields. The woman who brought me would leave me and the donkey and return to her domestic duties at home to prepare supper. I would lie around, tied up, waiting for the end of the day.

On the return trip home, my mother propped me up on the donkey, at the displeasure of the animal, and held me with adoration every step of the way home.

Chapter 2

LABOUR ON OUR ESTATE

On the farm the labour never ceased. Partial relief arrived in winter and on religious holidays; this is not to say that the entire town's folk were devoutly religious. It was just a way to pause from the heavy, long hours of farm labour. It was a time to rest and socialize in the town square.

A women's work was never done. There were many chores in the winter season for the women. There was mending and sowing clothing for the whole family. They made sandals called "peenchy" (similar to sandals worn by the North American Indians). These sandals were in place of shoes and were only worn on special occasions and holidays.

Other chores for the women included milking the cows, preserving peppers, baking bread and constantly cooking for our large household.

I can't remember what occupied the men in the winter season except the annual slaughter of the pig that had been fattened up all year for the occasion.

My Uncle George single-handedly operated a combined hardware store and stove manufacturing business which served the towns and the villages in the surrounding area. My other uncles and my father were over in Canada labouring and saving for the future.

My mother taught me to walk at age two and a half years old. The method of teaching was simple. She would call my name "Elia!" (the name I was Christened with) and hold her hands up. She commanded me to walk towards the wall (a total length of four feet). I obeyed my mother. I felt like a teddy bear with stiff legs as I accomplished the task of walking the full distance. My mother was so proud. I felt so elated.

"That was it! I could walk!"

I don't recall needing any further walking lessons. Walking back into my mother's arms confirmed me as a walker. Thereafter there was no big fuss made about of my first walking attempt.

Before I realized I was being registered for school. I was five or six years old and there was no such thing as a kindergarten class. I went straight into Grade One. I started memorizing the alphabet, writing plus arithmetic. History was taught in Grade Three or Four. But it was evident by the pictures of the Greek heroes surrounding the walls of the classroom, placed there to pique your curiosity and familiarize you with the faces of Alexander the Great, Pericles, Plato, Aristotle, etc.

One day when I was exiting the school doors, a group of children pointed at me yelling, "There's another one."

Before I realized I was wrestling with the school bully. My textbooks went flying and I was on my back, looking at the sky.

"Hurray!" the kids yelled, as they witnessed another victory for the bully.

"Who's next?" he cried.

Many years later I got my revenge on that guy. I married his niece!

Chapter 3

MY DISMAL ACADEMIC SCHOOL CAREER

School was my nemesis. As a child I developed low self-esteem, directly as the result of my academic career. Although my school sports activities during this time were fine, my school years had a profoundly negative effect on my life. How it started is a mystery. Perhaps it was a school mate commenting that I couldn't do something? I couldn't do things because I had not been shown how things were done. My mind must have jumped to the conclusion my classmates were born smart. They know how to do things. I had not figured out that it was because they had been taught.

I convinced myself whether it was reading, writing or arithmetic it could not be done by me. It was beyond my comprehension.

I could not shake the stigma. It became one of the biggest downfalls in my life. And the biggest effect it had on me was that because of this negative thinking I could never master English spelling, I felt that if I attempted I would surely fail.

I would not be writing this if not for the advent of the "spell checker" on my computer. It renders me the desire to write and the freedom from flipping the pages of the dictionary tracking down the correct spelling of a noun.

One advantage my academic insecurities bestowed upon me was I developed a vocabulary. By not knowing how to spell a specific word, I would mentally labour to find a noun that I could spell to fit in its place.

I did not develop a word picture in my mind. I was convinced that that was for smart people. It was not for me. If I tried, I would surely fail. Yet I must stress that I have always had a great desire to master learning.

I digress from my story because the subject matter has bothered me all my life.

Chapter 4

THE VILLAGE

Group entertainment came to our village once a year in the form of a movie. A very large, noisy projector was set up in the town square and at dusk the total community would be present. The majority of people would be standing, with the children sitting on the dusty ground. It was difficult to hear the story over the din of the projector. For two consecutive years, the same film was introduced by a picture of a lion roaring down on you from a screen placed very high so all could see.

At the age of five, viewing the movie for the first time in a very dark town square with no street lights was a frightening experience.

The movie was a religious presentation about the crucifixion of Jesus Christ. With the Roman soldiers nailing Jesus to the Cross, compounded with the introduction of that lion roaring down on you, it had a profound effect on a little boy.

When the crowd dispersed, you did not want to be seen escorted by your mother. Oh no, you had to walk home by yourself. Trudging up the hill to reach your domicile, you imagined the huge lion you saw on the screen lurking everywhere in the pitch-dark night.

I was luckier the second year. I had the light of a bright moon to guide me up the hill to the edge of town. I stayed in the middle of the mud road to avoid the shadows and saw only one stray pig. Hearing the oink and squeal of the animal I realized it was as frightened of the dark as much I was.

We lived on a hilltop overlooking the village with a river at the bottom. The river was well utilized by people washing clothes and irrigating the fields that were adjacent to the running river water.

I would often sit on the grassy hill, overlooking the women who were labouring over their washing. They would scrub and bash their clothing on rocks that were protruding out of the river.

One day as I sat watching, a boy who was eight or nine years of age, came up and sat down beside me. He said to me, "You are lucky. You're going to America. My uncle has just returned from working in Germania (Germany). He said there is going to be a big war. The

Germans have a powerful army. Hitler, their leader, said he wants taken over all of Europe."

In that part of the world, young and old were born with constant fear of war. The boy's statement sent a pain to the pit of my stomach and added to my concern. I was the only one in my family of four that my father had sent for, to live with him in Toronto. I did not wish to leave my mother, but my father was the head of family. When ordered to do something, we did so without question. War or no war, I was very sad.

Talking of frightening... back to my school days. I was always filled with stress when entering any school building.

At age eight or nine, my class was given a homework assignment. We had to memorize a poem. I applied myself very diligently that evening. I had it down pat and ran it through my mind constantly on the way to school the next morning. When it came time to recite the poem, the teacher asked who wanted to be first. Half of the class raised the hand. I didn't. I did not want first.

A little girl was chosen. Up she stood and rhymed off the poem. I silently followed her verbiage and thought, "I can do the same." Then the teacher asked who wanted to be next. I slowly put my hand up with a dozen other children, but I was not chosen. I followed along with the next child's presentation. He made a couple mistakes and the kids started laughing at him. This made me lose all confidence. The next boy the teacher pointed a finger to did not do well and the laughter followed. That's when I ceased volunteering. I thought that unless the teacher points a finger at me I wouldn't try. I spent the rest of the class hoping desperately she would not chose me and she didn't. I was so relieved and yet I walked home frustrated because I was so confident I could accurately repeat the memory assignment. Never again did I have confidence in any school project, which was my biggest academic downfall. (Unless, of course I was born with some deficiency that I have been bucking all these years and that I am not aware of.)

If I didn't feel like I had academic smarts, I did feel I had common-sense and street-smarts. I don't recall who advised me about this piece of medical advice but I think it was one of my pre-teen chums. If you received a scratch and you were bleeding, place some dry earth over it and it will stop bleeding and cure it. Not knowing what a Band-aid was in those days, (if it was invented that far back).

I recall trying this treatment once myself. I was away from home and I picked up a bit of dry earth and poured it onto my bleeding finger. The dry earth absorbed the red blood, congealed it and stopped the bleeding. It was an unsanitary procedure to say the least but I received no infection and no gangrene developed. It appeared to work and I didn't die.

The village of Zhelevo/Antartikon from the west mountain road leading to Prespa.

The older generation who knew my grandfather slighted him, they said I look like him.

Chapter 5

KICKED BY A MULE

When I was an infant riding on the donkey with my mother's constant support, I enjoyed her attention. But, when I learned to walk, that same donkey sent me flying with his two hind hooves.

I guess I was about eight or nine years of age, and old enough to do certain chores, when I was instructed to deliver the donkey to the field where the family was labouring on that particular, dull day.

The animal was taken out of the barn for me, and directed out onto the path leading to the field where the work was being performed by the family. I was instructed to follow the donkey, after all he has more experience and was older then I was. So there was nothing for me to do but follow the jackass. Leaving the edge of our town, I got bored and sleepy, so I leaned my head on the side of the donkey's rump as we were walking. A few minutes later the donkey was waving his tail across my head as a warning. Not paying any attention to that dumb donkey, with both his back hooves he delivered such a swift kick to my groin. Wooeee!

He sent me flying about four feet in the air. I hurt as much as I was surprised. While crying, I picked up a stick and I attacked that donkey. I landed one to his back side and he raced off. My family laughed because the donkey arrived at our destination long before I did. I never revealed what really happened that day. The above stands as my writing confession. Old people have a vivid memory of what experience they had far in their past. To recall what happened yesterday or last week comes with some difficulty. But I must say that from then on I developed the greatest respect for donkeys and their powerful high-kicking hooves.

Chapter 6

MANUFACTURING AND PREPARING FOOD

Each year, a pig is sacrificed for the family pork supply of meat for the year. Meat was a big treat. They were not aware of it at the time but limiting your meat intake leads to healthy life-style and medical research has also proved it extends your life.

We existed on bread from the wheat we harvested and baked ourselves right at the source. We sowed the seeds, grew the wheat and with a heavy, long handled sickle labouriously cut the wheat. Then we bundled the grain stalks, transported them by cart to the gumno, a field beside our house. The ground was prepared with cow dung that had been sun-dried. The wheat sheaves were laid down over this prepared round field and the donkey was set to work. Attached by rope to a pole in the middle, he stomped around in a circle, separating the kernels from the sheaves. When that was done we removed the sheaves and swept the wheat kernels into a sack, ready to be taken to the mill and converted into flour. I would say that this method is a little harder then going to the store for a loaf of bread!

Taking the flour home, we then added water and kneaded it by hand to make bread dough and then we baked the bread in our own home-made oven. This oven resembled a pizza oven in a present day pizza restaurant. Also we had no switch to turn on the oven. We had to find the wood and cut it to size to fit in the oven. It is quite a procedure to follow to eat a slice of bread, especially when the bread is baked in an oven a separate structure away from the house. Our oven was outside in our enclosed yard, adjacent to a storage room.

Once the bread was baked it was wrapped in cloth sheets to keep it fresh. We baked enough bread to last a month. The storage area was locked and sealed to prevent entry by rodents and creepy crawlies.

Feta was another staple of our meals. Feta is goat cheese manufactured by extracting milk from our own animals. A herd of goats and sheep were maintained at our out-of-town cottage or koliba (the Macedonian term). For a percentage of the yield, a man is hired to watch over the animals grazing in the fields, on this beautiful mountain area.

Each autumn, all the families who have these hired know-how people commence to process feta goat cheese and butter milk. It was a very busy two week period, for time seemed to be of the essence for production. Once made the cheese was stored underground in a cool place for preservation.

Come springtime, the families with those hired know-how people, would sheer sheep. The sheep were fed all winter in an enclosed area and had grown a great coat of hair which would be used to make clothing for the family.

Olives were another main staple to life in Macedonia. Olives were shipped from the south in exchange for our plentiful wheat growth.

The balance of food was consumed by the population on the basis of seasonal availability. Potatoes, corn, vegetables, etc. were eaten when they were grown. Grapes, before the bulk was converted into wine, were great with a slice of home-baked bread.

But, I have stalled long enough in relating the gruesome tale of the murder of the pig, which was fattened all winter for this purpose.

The preparation was to first invite a neighbour or a relative to aid you in this murderous affair. The long wicked knives were sharpened while the men discuss procedure of the attack. Then the poor animal was released in the wall-enclosed yard of the house while the children and the women of the house had the grandstand view on the high veranda.

We would watch with excitement mixed with sorrow for the pig, who I was sure had a feeling that he was the forthcoming Christmas feast. The pig would squeal to high heaven for mercy, while being chased around and around the yard by two or three adults stabbing him with long ferocious knives, the length of swords.

The men would honestly feel sorry for the poor animal and attempt to quickly put an end to the poor creature's life (and to squelch the loud squealing). This torture would take about a half hour. To a boy of six or eight this event would lead to endless, sleepless nights. It was a shock to say the least.

The deed was done, the butchers would proceed to cut up the carcass in different portions. They skinned the pig with short, curved, sharp knives, being very careful with the skin as it was very valuable. It was converted into moccasins for the family. The liver and kidneys were used for food as well as the entrails for casings for making sausages. The other parts of the body were portioned-off and stored, and would appear on the dinner table when we had special visitors.

That evening, the women of the house, cooked some portion of the killed animal fat. It would melt and drip into a pot that would be saved for cooking. What was left was served to the butchers, and a sample was given to us children. Every morsel of the pig was utilized, except for the hooves, which you would see being carried off by the dogs.

Chapter 7

FASTING FOR JESUS

Easter is the biggest religious holidays of the Eastern Orthodox religion. A time to fast.

Boys somehow never, ever volunteered for the challenge of fasting. The young females would fast for a two-week period. They would assemble in groups and persevere. NO food, only water.

My sister and cousin participated one year and I recall, on my mother's instruction, going to our neighbour's house to view how my sister was surviving the fasting ordeal. The front door was wide open. The strongest body odour was permeating out of the room where those poor, starving souls were lying down to preserve their strength.

The women of the home spotted me and shooed me out, stating, I was not supposed to be there. When I was safely outside, I peeked in the window. My sister spotted me and came outside the front door, and told me to beat it, with a cold tone and then, with determination, hurled something in my direction, just missing me by inches. I reported to my mother that my sister was feeling alright and so was her throwing arm.

For many years after, I cannot remember such high stench exhuming from a group of young people, on a liquid diet. It smelled a lot in the room they all slept in and where they all kept a watchful eye over each other to make sure that no one sneaked in any food. What a sacrifice for the sake of our Eastern Orthodox religion.

Chapter 8

EASTER HOLIDAYS

The two churches of the town were saturated with people inside and outside and all around the church premises. Every person, young and old, held a lit candle in front of him. The icons on the walls were adorned with three and four large tall white candles.

There was no fear of a fire because they were in the house of God. It was a miracle because even at my tender age, holding my candle, with parishioners overhead with their candles it felt that all the oxygen seemed to be extracted making it difficult to breathe.

The midnight Easter service was not complete until the Priest, carrying a large cross, headed out of the church's main door with altar boys and the congregation following him. Around the church he walked three times chanting "Christos Anestis" in Greek, which means "Christ has risen, Christ has risen, Christ has risen."

It was one minute past midnight and there we were, young and old, all repeating as we circled the church three times. It was a chilly bright night, with the stars shining and the moon over-powering all. The stiff breeze made it difficult to keep our candles lit and we cupped the flame of the candle together as we walked around the church. When a person's flame went out, they would borrow a light from the person walking beside him.

You could see in the dark towards our neighbouring town people walking with blazing candles, poring out of their church. It looked kind of spooky and ghoulish to a young kid. This was emphasized at that precise moment by a town's ruffian pointing and saying, "There he is, Jesus Christ has risen. He is flying to God." with a little smirk in his voice.

At the end of the service, we all walked to our individual homes with our lit candles. As you entered the house and your candle was still lit, you would make a complete round of the home, making the sign of the Cross in each corner and room. Then, we proceeded with a midnight supper.

My cousin and sister, who had participated on the two-week diet, were praised, although they were too weak to attend the Easter church service. However they commenced to gorge themselves with food. We, the children, were then permitted to compete and play the game of cracking the Easter eggs. This was long awaited. Kids would talk about this and crave this activity. Eggs were a scarce commodity in those days and therefore a big treat for little people as well as for the adults.

The next morning, we dressed in our finest attire, and we would return to church, which was not as crowded as the night before during midnight mass.

(What follows next is a kid's view, from someone under the age of ten.)

Following the afternoon Church service, the whole congregation walked to the river, with the Priest leading the congregation, holding the Holy Cross chanting and waiving with it, blessing each house along the way.

Arriving at the river the Priest selected the deepest part of the fast running river located at the back of the wheat mill where the water gorged out and prevented it from freezing in the centre. Ice was visible along each side of the fast running water.

The Priest stood on a ledge attached to the wall of the wheat mill. He commenced his chanting and waving of the Cross. The congregation watching the Priest as he made the sign of the Cross and they immediately followed chanting, "Christos Anestis". Christ has risen, Christ has risen, and then replied, "Alethos anesti". "It is true he has risen. It is true he has risen. It is true he has risen." Which was frequently repeated.

I was corrected and told by my sister, to do it right (the sign of the Cross), "Not once, not twice, but three times, Stupid."

I followed her wishes, and moved away from her, for relief, and a better view of the river.

Chapter 9

HERO WORSHIP

My first heroes that I so envied were the young men of 15-to-20 years of age, standing (wearing their Sunday-best clothing) in a row on each side of the icy-cold mountain water during a ceremony that took place during the Feast of the Holy Theophany each January 6th.

I remember watching as the water gushed down out of the mouth of the mill, creating white foam while swirling to find its route down-river, between the ice along the banks.

Six or eight young men [heroes in my eyes] fully-clothed ready and anxiously waiting sized up their opponents. Some picked a higher ground while others climbed a huge riverside bolder to dive into that bitter cold water all for the honour of retrieving the Holy Cross. But they had to wait until the Priest finished his sermon before he tossed the Cross into the deepest section of a vicious, bone-chilling torrent of river water. Oh how I envied those guys ready to dive for the Holy Cross!

I was particularly sad because I had learned that I would never have the opportunity to compete for the highest prize in the land, since my mother had told me that soon I would have to go and live in America (as it was called) with my father.

Finally, the Priest kissed the Cross and tossed it in the water.

Before the Cross touched the fast flowing deep water, the young divers were airborne, diving into the icy river water. The heavy Cross rapidly sunk to the bottom of that freezing river. That's when the excitement commenced. They had to dive and forage for the Cross in the deepest foam section of the river which made it difficult to spot. At times they looked like a relay team, because some had to come up for air while the others frantically searched for the Holy Cross. If two competitors simultaneously laid hands on the Cross, a vicious tug of war commenced while the two floated to the surface. If one could stay longer underwater, holding his breath and on to the Cross, he won.

In the meantime, the mothers of the competitors, holding dry clothing, were crying and having very stressful moments.

Once the winner climbs out of the water he presents the bearded old Priest the wet Cross. The Priest acknowledges the winner by reaching over with his first finger making the sign of the Cross on the winner's forehead.

That day I did not hear hands clapping from the people in attendance, maybe the din of the water gorging down from the mill drowned any noise or ovations. The winner, like those before him, received NO prize. The honour of retrieving the Cross was the prize and his name being briefly mentioned in the next Church service.

The only thing I viewed was the mother of the winner, waiving to him with dry clothing in her arms. By the time he reached his Mother, most of the other competitors were coming out of the bushes already wearing their dry clothing and running home to sit in front of a warm fire, which was the method used to ward-off a cold or worse, pneumonia, I have never heard of anyone dying after such a heroic deed. The good Lord above watches over them.

I once asked what if the Cross could not be retrieved? The answer I received was that the Priest would have to dive in the water and keep searching until he finds the Holy Cross. No one has ever heard of a Priest diving to retrieve a Cross.

Chapter 10

MY ONE AND ONLY SWIMMING LESSON

One summer day, I wondered where all the kids had gone. Along came a school chum who told me the kids were at the river, swimming,
"That's where I am going," he said.
"Oh!" I said, disappointedly, "I can't swim."
I was seven or eight years old and had not been taught.
"Come on, I'll teach you," he offered.
We got to the swimming hole which was located at a bend in the river with trees and shrubs to conceal our whereabouts from our parents. There were about 10 boys all bare-naked, no body hair on anyone, frolicking around. Clothes were parked on boulders and on shrubs. Kids were swinging from low lying branches. This was a very private swimming hole with a rocky, slippery bottom.

The chilly water flowed down from the snow-capped mountain gurgling over the rocks, muffling the kids yelling.

By the time I removed my clothing, my swimming teacher was in the cold-water waving to me to come in. As I approached him, we were shoulder-high in that chilly, cold water.

"Now (sega) I'll show you how to swim. Hold your breath and put your head underwater."

I did what I was told.

"Now," he said, "Move your arms sideways and kick your legs up and down,"

I followed his instruction and he then said, "Now you can swim!" and immediately took off to play with the other boys. I never saw him again. There I was with goose bumps all over me, bobbing up and down in that cold mountain water, repeating his brief lesson over and over again in my head. A short while later someone's mother screamed, "There they are!" We all quickly dispersed.

Arriving home, my nose was running and I was sniffling, I had to confess to Mother I was at the swimming hole, but everything was all right. I could swim now. She gave a pat on the rump and a hug. She then put me down and covered me to sleep.

Chapter 11

THE TOWN'S BLACKSMITH

Our town had the distinction of having a blacksmith. Many people from surrounding villages around our mountainous area made tracks to our town to purchase leather goods for themselves and horseshoes and saddles for their domestic animals.

The town's blacksmith was a master at creating saddles for horses and donkeys. For three days of the week he did the circuit of the villages to apply his craft and the rest of the time he was in his shop. When he was in his shop the boys would line up waiting their turn to pump the hearth to a high heat which would be used to soften the steel. The steel would then be placed on the anvil and formed into a horseshoe by creating holes for the nails [two on each side] for attaching on the hoof of the animal.

It was late afternoon and the sun was rapidly setting on our town located between two mountains. I was the last in line to have a turn. Some of the kids who were waiting had got inpatient or their mothers had called, ordering them home. I stayed. My mother could not see me from our house on the hill. At last, I reached for the handle of the long thick wooden rod leading to the hearth. It was attached to a leather bag with a wide mouth. As one pumped the long rod (in a motion like an accordion) air blew on the hot fire creating sparks and blue flames.

I pumped and pumped as I watched the blacksmith forming red-hot iron rods on anvil with a heavy hammer while creating a tune unlike any other instrument I had ever heard. I was mesmerized watching an artist at work. He actually did not view his accomplishment as art. He did not stand back and admire what he had done. A completed task to him was just labour he had performed many times. It was a livelihood.

Time flies when a kid is absorbed. The afternoon was quickly overpowered by pitch-black darkness, I was afraid to step out into it. I heard too many ghoulish stories to feel any comfort making my way up the hill to my home. When I got in, Mother asked me where I was so late at night. My sister had noticed me in line at the blacksmith shop, and quickly it blurted out. Thanks Sis. That girl never liked me because I was male and she wished she had been born one.

My Eyes Have Seen

Chapter 12

TRUCK STUCK IN THE MUD

The total amount of personal automobiles in this town of mine was exactly none. There was only one mode of transport; a huge truck that was utilized for everything including carrying vegetables, fruit and wheat to the mill. It could be converted to a taxi or a bus by adding a long wooden bench to the centre and a bench on each side of the truck when the occasion demanded.

This transport vehicle serviced many towns and villages in the area since it had a captive audience. When owning your vehicle (as my uncle did) it was necessary to be able to repair and service the four wheel steel monster yourself. You had to know what made it move, because there were no repair shops close by. If one was not mechanically inclined, one did not venture into the transport business. Luckily, my uncle was a mechanic.

His arrival schedule was known by all the people and children of the town. He would be spotted coming from distance in his truck; a novelty wood frame and steel machine structure on four wheels. It rumbled and swayed over the potholes of the so called highway and into the centre of town.

If you were expecting a parcel or any kind of delivery you would walk to the centre square and pick up your order from my uncle who had, at your request, purchased whatever you had asked for from the big city of Florina.

On rainy days, the kids of the town would yell with excitement, "The truck is coming. The truck is coming!"

The kids knew the location of the deepest portion of the road where the heavy mud gathered and settled following a rainy day. We would wait, with some adults observing as well, to see the big steel monster negotiate across a strip of the soft muddy road into town, creating a deep indentation of mud on a rainy day. We kids would cheer when the big truck got stuck up to the axles. This meant we could take off our shoes and socks and walk in that thick muck to help. I was always the first to render assistance. After all, the chauffeur (as he was called) was my uncle.

27

My uncle was a gentle giant of a man. He was displeased to see this gang of kids surrounding the vehicle on four sides, shouting orders at him to "Go forward!", "Go back!" and "Stop!"

The kids were drenched in mud as some pushed backwards while others would push forward. My poor uncle was terrified he would run over or hurt one of those kids. Many evenings when stuck in the mud, he would abandon the truck and go home to avoid the generous help the kids were ready and most willing to render. The next morning he would wait until the school building swallowed these helpful kids then he would proceed to dig his truck out of the mud with aid from a few adults.

Chapter 13

HOUSING THE LIVESTOCK
AND HARVESTING THE CROPS

Today we park our automobiles on our side drive or in the garage adjacent to our house. In my young days in Macedonia, we parked our live stock in our homes. The animals that were utilized for the day's labour at home or in the fields were the donkey, horse and cow. These creatures occupied the ground floor of the houses for two reasons; for convenience and instant availability and safety from someone borrowing them permanently. We humans occupied the second floor.

The sheep and goats in the field were watched over by a hired individual who has no livestock of his own. His payment for taking care of them was to receive two or three animals for his home to feed his family. A cottage, with a fenced off area for sheep, was available to this caretaker to spend the nights and provide safety from bears, wolves and thieves. The caretaker slept on the premises and was supplied with food and some form of firepower to ward off any intruders, animal or human.

The barter system worked quite well. When the wheat was ready for harvest there were people available for hire. They were also available for picking grapes and for the processing of cheese. Although it required a specialist to make cheese. No money transaction ever took place. All the employees were supplied a percentage of the annual yield.

I recall watching people churning butter milk in a long wooden container cylinder in shape. They would beat up and down with a pole that had the appearance of a mop. On one end of the pole was a piece of circular wood that was two or so inches smaller in circumference than the long three or 4 foot high bucket. People would move the pole up and down to create the buttermilk.

The only thing I can recall about the making of goat cheese was that it was placed in cloth to drip dry for a few days in order to create our delicious Feta cheese.

Sheering sheep was also a specialty that one had to have a knack for. The task, I recall in the evenings at home, was often the topic of discussion as to who should be selected to that job.

All labour had its season before the harsh winter snow descended on us. We imitated the bees. Each year you must do the labour, sow the seeds and water and nurture them, when the time is right, with haste one must bring in the crops to eat in the winter.

As with the other work, the barter system was also used for paying the wages of any person who assisted with the stocking and storing provisions for the long cold winter season. When the snow silently arrived it covered both sides of our mountains with our village at the bottom. That wind and snow blowing between the mountains covered the village rendering it immobile for humans or beasts.

Chapter 14

THE TOWN SQUARE

The town square was used for most events and it was there for everyone to use. If there was a wedding, everyone headed for the town square for the horo [line dance] portion of the wedding reception. Everyone was expected to participate in the town square. There was no secret who was married to whom. It was not necessary to publish the betrothal (even if we had a paper to do so) just be present at the town square on a Sunday, or any day of rest and you'd get the news.

It comes to mind of an event when a relative of ours was being married to a person from a neighbouring town. The wedding ceremony was performed in our church, followed by the traditional dance in our town square. Then the relatives mounted their horses and escorted the bride and groom to the neighbouring town called Oshchima where the reception was taking place. This was also where the bride and groom were planning take up residency with the groom's family.

My uncle mounted his steed ready to go with the bridal party.

He looked down on me and read my mind. He reached down to me with one arm and said, "Come on!"

He shouted to my aunt to tell my mother I was going with him to the wedding.

"Okay, hold on" he said, "And don't fall down."

And away we rode on horseback with the bridal party.

I cannot remember that horse travel, as I was too busy hanging on to my uncle, as he instructed me to do.

When we arrived there were live musicians playing in their town square greeting us and then escorting us to the reception. I sat with the grown up party. I could not see any other kids.

We dined and gave a toast to the bride and groom. Each guest, began with a toast to the bride and groom, as he had his first shot of rackia (home-made whiskey),. All the guests would raise their shot glass chanting the same words over and over again. My uncle was having a good time and was feeling no pain. The rackia, Ouzo and wine kept flowing.

Shortly after the food was consumed, my uncle instructed me to make my way back home, while there was daylight left. I commenced walking on a goat path (the short cut to my village). There was a group of people ahead of me but soon disappeared from my view. The dusk turned into night. I stayed on the narrow hilly path hoping it would lead me to my destination. I finally reached the village and was found by my mother. We walked home with much relief to both of us and to a welcomed wide mattress where my mother, sister, brother and I slept.

Chapter 15

AMERICA BOUND

The time had arrived for me to leave everything, and everyone, I knew me behind. The pit of my stomach felt hollow. I was going to America (Toronto, Canada) to live with my father. The reason why, I was told by my mother, was because he was lonely, I didn't even know my father. I recall meeting him briefly once, about a year previously. At that time, I was told by someone not to be too friendly with my father because he was going to take me with him to America. So I kept my distance from my father. At the time my grandmother and the family begged him not to take me, saying that the boy (I) was too young.

I didn't want to go. I did not dwell on that thought at all or I would have taken off to live in those beautiful high mountains of my village.

But instead I had to follow orders from the head of my family. Besides strong boys don't cry, I was told. And I tried to be one, for my mother's sake.

Unbeknownst to me, the passport and travel vouchers had been pre-arranged months ago. The family waited until I finished the school year, which was June, 1933, then Mother sent me to say good-bye to my teacher. She lived in a corner house on the second floor.

Walking to the teacher's house, I felt great trepidation as I passed a little girl's house. I remembered that a while back she had thrown a stone at me while she was standing on the edge of a steep hill. She slipped and fell, rolling down the steep hill. Luckily a shrub stopped her. She started crying and screaming, "He pushed me and tried to attack me!"

Thank goodness, her mother witnessed the whole incident, otherwise I would have been in big trouble.

That same little girl spotted me on the way to the teacher's house. She waved to me and stuck her tongue out at me. I pretended not to see her and made haste to enter the teacher's residence. The lady greeted me, saying, "Elia (my Macedonian name), I am going away also."

She was busily packing to go south, to stay with her mother for the summer.

Then the teacher, Ms Choula, gave me my grade four passing certificate (which I didn't deserve) with instructions to give it to the school
I would be attending in September.

"Also, they have Greek schools in America, so remember to finish
your Greek schooling in America."

She advised me not to forget my people or the country I was born
in. "Be a good boy, obey your father."

She said good bye, and sent me on my way.

On the way home, that troublesome little girl, waived to me, to get
my attention then stuck her tongue out again at me, saying goodbye to
me her own way. I kept walking while I watched as a gift of a flying rock
came from her direction. Later that day, informing my mother of the
experience I had with that nasty little girl, she said, "Ah! She likes you.
Don't pay any attention to her."

Chapter 16

THE SAD DAY OF MY EXODUS

That morning the family permitted me to sleep in as long as possible. Finally, my sweet, heart-broken mother gently awakened me saying, "It's time to get dressed." She was taking care, avoiding verbalizing "You are leaving here and this town for good, son."

I reciprocated in kind by saying to myself, "Big boys don't cry."

Of course it was easy for me to conform. The shock of me leaving rendered me oblivious to everything.

I remember being helped getting dressed, but can't recall what clothing I wore, new or old. They gave me something to eat. The next stage was my whole family, including my grandmother, my uncle, my two aunts, my two male cousins, my three female cousins, and my one sister, and my six-year-old brother, (all whom I lived with all my life), escorting me through the town. All, except my sister.

As I walked through the town I would say good bye to "her" here, and "him" there. People of the town stood in front of their open doors waving good bye to me. People were gently saying and waving good bye to me or otherwise they would not even acknowledge me if I passed them on the street. I felt as if I was in a funeral procession and I was the deceased. I was unhappy. I was leaving my village with a heavy heart. I did not want to cry, it would upset my dear mother. Besides, I repeated to myself again and again, "Big boys don't cry."

Then my two married aunts came out of their homes crying and hugging me good bye, chanting greetings to my father and uncles in America. One of my aunts joined the family parade and accompanied my dear crying mother to the city of Florina, located on the other side of our mountain. I was being escorted to board the train and leave the country and my village forever.

We reached the dusty highway and the edge of the town with my entourage and a few other people waiting to board the forthcoming transport, ending the long de-stressing walk from my home. I felt like a zombie walking to the outskirts of town, arriving on the dirt highway with many deep potholes.

While waiting, my grandmother (Baba) took out a pocket knife and instructed her son, my uncle, to go to a little wood bridge that spanned a little creek and remove a large splinter of wood. My uncle quickly went and when he returned he gave it to his mother. She then placed it on a red handkerchief and Baba, that dear old lady, holding this large sliver of wood on the palm of her hand, said to me, "You are going to cross a great body of water, on a big chunka (boat). When you get on board and it starts sailing you will go to the side of the ship and throw this piece of wood overboard, and say, 'I will get you before you get me.' This shall prevent you from getting seasick."

"All right, Babo." I replied, as she placed it in my satchel.

"Don't forget!"

"I won't," I said to my grandmother.

Still waiting for the transport on the highway on the edge of town I would never see again, I was stunned out of my wits. In the distance we viewed a moving dust bowl on the mountain road heading in our direction. It was my other uncle, the chauffeur. Ten minutes or so later he appeared. He disembarked with two men and the three of them approached me. My uncle, the chauffeur, said to me, pointing to and endorsing their presence, "These two men are coming with you to America!" Then he introduced them to me by their first names.

Having older travel companions seemed like a good idea, even if they were strangers from another village. My uncle continued, "These good men will take you to your father." They both nodded their heads in agreement.

We boarded the back of the truck. The two men sat in the front cab with my uncle. In the back, with my two pieces of luggage, was me, my mother and my aunt, who accompanied my mother in her sorrow.

The large truck that day was equipped with a long wood bench, extending from one side to the other of the tall canvas-covered vehicle. In the centre of this high long vehicle at our feet, he had placed bushels of vegetables, sacks of corn and wheat and machine parts for delivery.

Before I boarded, my gentle loving grandmother, with tears in her eyes, said "I won't be going with you to the train station in Florina city. I am too old to travel."

She hugged me. "Tell your father and uncles not to worry about us. We are all fine." At that moment my eyes watered but I held back from crying out loud. I kept hugging my dear, dear Baba.

Boarding the transport truck we drove a short distance out of the village. We had one more ceremony to perform.

The vehicle stopped at an icon on the side of the road. My aunt and my mother Nenka disembarked and lit a candle placed it in front of the icon, with a picture of Mary holding her son Jesus. They cried softly. I was left on the truck. We all made the sign of the Cross then somebody said a few words regarding a safe journey.

We then proceeded on our sad way. The vehicle struggled up the dusty single lane highway.

Sitting in the back of the truck, my mother, my aunt and I, with the supplies, lumbered and swayed with each huge pothole, and there were many of them. We passengers had to hold onto the open wood boards to stay on the narrow bench, while the truck was negotiating up each steep hill and straining the screeching breaks on the decline on the other side of the steep mountain.

My uncle covered this road two to three times a week, in rain, sleet and heavy snow, year-round, hauling goods, loading and unloading material to stores and homes. He was dedicated. This was his livelihood and he was a very hard working man. The people of the village envied him because he was the grand possessor of a broken-down, creaky, old truck. We arrived at the little city of Florina Train Station. My two adult companions disappeared somewhere. My uncle had some deliveries to make in the city so they left us three at the station. My dear mother could not hold on any longer. She broke down crying. My aunt consoled her.

A while later my uncle returned to say good-bye to me and he assured me again I would be alright travelling with these two older men. "They will take you directly to your father, and say health to your father and uncles for me. Thank them for their financial help in purchasing my truck."

We shook hands. I had a feeling I would never see him again.

Then he gave my aunt (his wife) and my mother instructions to wait for him at the train station for the trip back home to the village [thinking to myself "without me"]. There was a deep depression in that thought as I watched his huge truck turning the corner on his way to complete his deliveries. Compounded with my poor mother crying, at distance away from my view to avoid me seeing her pain, it was a terrible ordeal for both of us. Then the transport driver drove off in his truck and without looking back my uncle had disappeared in to thin air.

The pain must have been so great because I cannot remember anything else about my goodbyes to those two women. I can recall, however, my two travelling companions at the doorway helping me on the train and me sitting in the train compartment opposite them. And, I remember, the train in motion.

Some hours later, we disembarked in the city of Thessalonika, the second biggest city in Greece. This was my first exposure to the very busy streets and long buses with steel wheels running on train tracks (streetcars).

We stopped at an outside café. They asked me what I wished to eat but I was too depressed to consume anything. We checked into a hotel and my two companions went out to supper. I was alone in a small room, watching the very busy traffic. The sidewalks were jammed with humanity. Inside the over-crowded streetcars people were packed like sardines in a can. The front and rear cow-catchers, where people would get off and others would jump on, were full. I had never seen anything like it before. I was fascinated at how people managed not to slip-off and get crushed to death under those huge, noisy steel wheels.

The next morning we had breakfast a few feet from the hotel in front of a café on a busy side walk. We had a sesame bun in the shape of a large thin dry bagel. Then we proceeded to a building, climbed up three flights of stairs, and went into an office where we sat together. We answered numerous questions and I can't remember whether it was a government office or a travel agency.

The thing I do remember was the three of us with the interviewer, who was carrying sheets of paper, crossing a very busy street and entering another office on the main floor of a larger building. He stamped the sheets of paper he was carrying, then handed them to us and we walked out of the building by ourselves.

I think that same day we boarded the train, leaving the country that held my beautiful village nesting between two mountains.

Leaving one's birthplace for most of us is permanent. You may return someday to visit relatives in the holiday season, if the work you are shackled to permits you the extra time to cover the distance or if your funds permit the long voyage.

Chapter 17

CROSSING EUROPE

When crossing the great continent of Europe, my depression prevented me from fully being able to appreciate the voyage. The countryside, the sound of the different languages at station stops, and the great cities was all wasted on a ten-year-old homesick boy.

The constant loud click of the wheels on the railway track speeding cross-country did not help my situation. It was a great relief when the train stopped at stations and the two gentlemen would venture out to the local food shop in the station for a sandwich or an orange, which, I think, was our means of sustenance across Europe.

Miles and miles of staring across the landscape of forest and farmland with barns and houses, passing towns and villages at a distance, as we left one country and entered another to the tune of that constant clicking of the wheels just increased my pain of homesickness. I knew those wheels were taking me further away from my village in the mountains of Macedonia. It depressed me to think I would never see my home again.

My travelling buddies struggled to speak a few words in every country we had a stop over in. I noticed they were straining with the French language when we reached Paris and had to transfer trains for one heading to the coast of France.

The big locomotive disgorged us with many other passengers on the coast, at the customs entrance which was the ship embarkation station. We had several hours of waiting there with half the time being consumed by customs and ship validation. When it was completed we found ourselves in an enclosed area, waiting for the ship.

Out from the grey blue ocean appeared to me a huge white castle, standing stationary, with its chimney stack emitting dark smoke. How could such a huge house stay afloat in the water?

My two travelling companions pointed to the ship saying, "That's what we shall be on to get to your father."

The tender boat we boarded to take us to this floating wonder shrunk to the size of a canoe, as it reached the ship. We floated up to a set of stairs that were bobbing up and down with the help of the sea. Sailors were available to help us up those swaying steel stairs and onto a landing leading into the ship. We lined up and a man, with an official sounding voice called out the names and handed us key to our cabin.

The name of the ship was "The Empress of Britain" and its origin was England. It picked up European passengers off the coast of Cherbourg, France, where we boarded her for a 7-day trip across the Atlantic Ocean bound for Halifax, Nova Scotia, Canada.

When we reached our cabin I immediately saw there were two double-tier bunks. I was given the upper of one side while the other upper bunk bed we used to store our suitcases. It was great. I had a ladder to climb to my bunk bed with a rod that pulled up across the width of the bed to protect you from rolling off when sleeping.

After settling in, we toured our deck to let me become familiar with where we were and where I could go. I was instructed that when I was by myself I was to remain on that deck only.

Shortly thereafter the fog horn blew three loud blasts and I could hear the anchor chains freeing the ship to float. I instantly made a bee-line for my cabin and dashed back up on deck by the railing. I unwrapped the contents of a handkerchief and threw that piece of wood into the water and mumbled these words "I will get you before you get me."

I felt relief obeying my grandmother's instructions. I can candidly say, I cannot remember if I suffered with seasickness or not.

I was off on the first sea venture of my life. I was going to live on the Ocean for a whole week before we see land again. A little scary, all that deep blue sea below me.

We were designated a table in the dining room for the duration of the voyage. In the huge dining area all the tables were covered with white linen and all the formal dinnerware was set for the evening, while a piano was played gently in the background.

Not knowing the English language and the waiter standing and waiting for my order made it somewhat intimidating for this ten-year-old boy, so that first night I requested, through my travelling companion interpreters, "fried eggs." From then on for the total journey, unless something else was placed before me to eat, if asked, I would reply "Fried eggs."

One day on deck I was watching the deep blue ocean bobbing the ship up and down. An English gentleman came and stood beside me and started to talk. Realizing I didn't really understand what he was saying, he brought out a ten-cent coin, and gestured and said "If you come to my cabin I will give you more money."

My travel companions had told not to go with or speak to strangers, so I accepted his coin and walked away from him. I told my buddies what transpired and they said that I did the right thing. We never saw that English stranger again.

Third day out on the deep Atlantic Ocean, I was struck by the fact that no matter how humongous our ocean liner was, there was no doubt about who was the master of the sea. Our ship was tossed around like a cork and many times we walked the deck with a life jacket. It was mandatory until the "all clear" signal was announced over the loud-speakers.

Finally, far in the distance, we sighted land! A welcome sight to all the passengers who whopped and hollered with joy! It took until the following day to reach the port of Halifax, Nova Scotia, CANADA, the country, unknown to me. My fate had dictated to become my home territory for the rest of my life. It was now my duty to be loyal to my adopted country, and if necessary, defend it. But as my teacher had told me, no one should forget his roots. And as I came to learn, it adds stability and substance to life.

Some hours before touching shore, a little speed boat approached and a group of men boarded the ship. They were personnel from Canadian immigration and were sent to process the passengers before permitting us to land. My travelling companions told me if we didn't pass they wouldn't permit us entry into the country. I silently wished they would send us back to my village.

Our passports were stamped aboard ship, and we were issued an entry form to hand-in before leaving the docks. We transferred our suitcases onto the train parked along the dock side that was waiting for passengers disembarking off the ship.

It didn't seem long before we were clicking down the tracks in that locomotive with the familiar irritating click of the steel wheels.

My travelling buddies said "Two more days now and then you will see and be with your father."

That comment sent me wondering if I would recognize him or would he recognize me? We had not seen each other except briefly two years ago when he was home on holidays. And at that time I was instructed to keep my distance from him because he was preparing to take me to America.

Chapter 18

DOCKING IN HALIFAX – CANADA

I remember hearing that this was the land of promise of riches by many of my people in my village. However, my heart cries out for my Macedonian people, who were so ill prepared for a venture to North America. They had no understanding of the language, of the culture, plus no formal education, nor the financial resources to survive and take advantage of the opportunities that Canada had to offer. In retrospect, for the first generation of Macedonian immigrants living in Canada life was pure survival. It was a lifetime of struggle to simply exist with very little personal satisfaction.

I am cognizant of the sacrifice made my grandfather and father in order to make life easier for us in the newfound land. A very brave but perhaps some might consider to be a foolhardy decision to have one's own life sacrificed for his children future.

I consider my father a very unselfish soul to make the decision in the height of 1930s depression have me immigrate at the age of ten. (He did not have the financial means to bring all three of us in his family to Canada at the same time.) He chose me because he feared if I got any older, I would be stuck speaking English all my life with a foreign accent in Canada. In that period of the depression, my father's restaurant business was in a precarious state of affairs having difficulty meeting the rent.

Back to my tale...

Travelling westward on the Canadian National Railways, I viewed wide-open uncultured rocky landmass as far as I could see. The train tracks cut through heavy forest areas reaching vast tracks of cultivated fields and sparsely dotted hamlets and villages along the way.

Our first stop was in the province of Quebec in the cities of Montreal and Quebec City to purchase sandwiches and fruit. It was a hot July day and there were a few brief stops along the way to disembark and embark passengers. One interesting observation was that even the locomotives and the passenger compartments in this country appeared to me larger and higher.

The English language sounded very strange, flat and fast. My travel buddies commented to me, "You will be able to speak it (English) in a very short time. Your new friends will teach you when you play with them."

Those comments somehow put me at ease and I never gave speaking English any more concern.

On the second or third day of rail travel, the locomotive chugged into Union Station in Toronto. My father was not there to meet me. No one was there. As the three of us carried our suitcases from the train into the huge main waiting concourse in the Station, I still didn't spot my father. We then proceeded to the street to hail a taxi. My travelling buddies had an address to dispatch me to. It was early evening and ready to rain.

We spotted a cab. On approaching it, he said he is engaged. While we stepped back to look for a taxi, we were approached by a girl. She said a few words to us which I didn't understand. She then led us to her mother, who was holding on to a boy and a girl. She spoke to us in Macedonian and introduced herself. As she hugged and kissed me she said "I am your Aunt Keta and these are your cousins Helen, Alex and Sophia."

These were the first people I had the honour to meet and whom I have had a life-long association with. My aunt shook hands with my two travelling companions and invited them home for some refreshment. She then pointed to the waiting taxi. We piled our suitcases in the trunk and we all squeezed into the taxi and drove off to her humble, rented home at 88 Niagara Street in Toronto.

When we got there, my aunt sat my two friends side by side, served them refreshment, and then proceeded to ask them many questions about the old country and just news in general, while my cousin Alex was trying to amuse me.

Night fell, my father arrived. He greeted me with a hug and kiss on the cheek while I was sitting on a chair. He had a little conversation with my travelling companions. He thanked them very much and quietly slipped each one an honorarium in appreciation for escorting me on the journey.

Then they said good bye to us and they remarked that tomorrow they would be looking for employment but for now they were off to stay with relatives. They shook hands with me and said they'd see me again.

I am sad to say my path never crossed with those two gentlemen ever again. I would guess they were both in their mid-twenties. I guess our age differential permitted no common ground to make the effort to meet again. I really knew nothing about them except that they were anxious to find employment in the new world. Perhaps they had returned to their village in Macedonia for a holiday. Or maybe they went back to find a wife and get married, then they migrated back to the new world, saved money and then brought back the new bride and settled down for life.

To my young mind they represented a long invisible rope and if I could talk to them and keep pulling the line I would reach my village and touch every thing in it. That was sacred in my life.

Chapter 19

LIFE IN A STRANGE NEW WORLD

My aunt's rented house on Niagara Street in Toronto housed her family of six which included my aunt and uncle, their two girls and two boys plus me. My Aunt Keta did not need the extra burden on her shoulders, but accepted her responsibility cordially.

The house was located in an area which contained a mixture of industrial and residential buildings. We lived across the street from a mattress manufacturing factory. My uncle Basil attempted to work in that factory, handling the material used for stuffing mattresses but his lungs would not tolerate it. The working conditions forced to terminate his employment.

Next door to the mattress factory was an abattoir that supplied fresh killed meat to the city. The only family man from our village who was lucky enough to obtain employment at the abattoir was Mr. Nicoloff. He was the envy of the others because of his job. But he was a hard worker and came home every night with a blood-splattered leather apron. I would watch him as he quietly walked to the back door of his rented house, which faced his work place.

It must be noted here the reason my uncle Basil and Mr. Nicoloff found employment was that they were capable of haphazardly filling out an employment application and were lucky enough to be hired on the spot.

On the other side of the meat factory were the railway tracks where the live animals were unloaded and herded into the factory to be prepared for slaughter.

At the north east corner of Niagara St. and Bathurst St. was a junk yard. It was fenced off on two sides with the fence reaching from one building to the other. The junk yard contained corroded steel sheets, rusted auto body sections, machine parts, etc. It was operated by a Jewish man with long beard and in cold weather he could be seen huddled over a bon fire warming himself.

I would often watch him go out on his open wagon with a long seat in front of this deep wood box. The wagon was drawn by a tired unhappy horse and the two of them would troll the streets and alleyways of the city looking for iron and used discarded steel materials.

Adjacent to the junk yard on the Bathurst Street side was an old four-storey structure housing the famous Laura Secord Candy Factory. We did not know of any Macedonian employed in that company.

The great handicap my people had was because of their inability to read, write or speak English they were unable to complete a simple application form. This, compounded with fractured pride and low self esteem, was a stumbling block in seeking humble employment.

There were other Macedonian families living on our street who had migrated from our village. I guess it was truly "birds of a feather flock together" syndrome. This togetherness gave them a little comfort and encouragement to struggle forward for their survival. They left the old country and took a huge step back in the hope of two steps forward; if not themselves, at least for their children.

My four cousins were wonderful. They accepted me in the family as one of their own. We argued like brothers and sisters and as we got older I became more devoted to them, and they to me.

To help save money on fuel for cooking our meals, my cousin Alex and I regularly went to the train tracks with pails in hand looking for hunks of coal that would fall out of the boxcar trains. While boarding passengers at Union Station, the locomotives would fill up with water and coal and as the train chugged along the track the coal would roll off.

We had to compete with other boys for this precious commodity. If we didn't go early enough we would come home with empty pails.

The milk delivery in the mornings I found interesting. In the winter season, on extra cold days, the milk would freeze and protrude above the silver seal. The glass bottle would wear it like a cap.

Speaking of milk, once a year for a two-week period The Royal Winter Fair would take place at The Canadian National Exhibition grounds. My cousin and I would have to get up at 5:00 a.m. with a pail and make our way across the railway tracks and stand in line in front of a man milking the cows to get half a pail of milk. This was if we were lucky to be amongst the first waiting in line. We had to be very careful carrying it home. Gathering that fresh, warm, unpasteurized milk saved

After my recent arrival from northern Greece (circa 1934) with my Canadian cousins, the Trentons. A copy of this photo was sent to my mother in the old country to say "all is well".

Front row: on tricycle is Mike Trenton; centre row from left are cousin Sophie, aunt Keta, cousin Alexander; I am behind Sophie, cousin Helen is with hands on her mother Keta.

us from buying a couple of quarts from the milkman.

In those first few months I also met a few boys my age who, I assumed, had migrated from our village just a year or so earlier than I had. Their names were George Nicoloff, Tom Simmons and Jack Metanis. We were amongst the first from the old country who had taken residence in Canada in the Dirty 30's, at the height of the world's greatest depression. I marvel at how our parents accomplished such a feat. What a great sacrifice they made. There was so much stress on the man that supported a family during that time. He walked, fearing the sky would fall on him and that fear lived with him night and day. Yet the majority survived the trauma. We were a hardy race, very few could not tolerate the strain and stress and only one person I knew of (who sadly had a mental disability) returned to the humble life style on the village farm in Macedonia.

But a father's struggle for survival in his adopted country was also felt by his offspring. They would aid the parent in any meagre business the father was lucky enough to get involved with.

Many of our Macedonian people were forced into businesses of their own mainly to create a job for themselves because they could not find work. This was not just because of the depression. As I mentioned earlier, because of their lack of knowledge of written or spoken English, they were operating under a severe handicap. But in a business of their own they felt they could survive. To counteract their handicap, they could emphasize fast service, answering the few customers they had with YES, SIR / NO, SIR / COME AGAIN, SIR.

Remember, in those days E.S.L. (English as a Second Language) schools were not available to teach newcomers the English language.

Chapter 20

A DEGREE IN THE SCHOOL OF HARD KNOCKS

It was an interesting situation that many immigrants found themselves in. They were forced to enter a business of their own but they had no knowledge of how to operate a business. They were forced to develop (often by using their plain common sense) and gain useful knowledge in order to improve and eventually prosper. The age-old thought of "Necessity is the Mother of Invention" found many immigrants needing to go into some form of retailing whether it was owning a restaurant, shoe shining (which was popular in those days), knife sharpener, or storefront window-washer. Basically any enterprise the English immigrant would not stoop to undertake was an opportunity for my people arriving in Canada with no knowledge of the English language.

The Italians opened a retail fruit stores while my people, the Macedonians and Greeks opened greasy spoons they called restaurants. They earned experience by first washing dishes and watching the cook. Eventually they would take his place on his day off. Then, they would bus dishes in the dining room and soon filling in for the waiter on his day off.

After this vast experience, the immigrant now thinks he is ready to open his own restaurant. That is when his real education and his heartaches commence. The success rate of these greasy spoons was very low. Those that did survive were forced to stay in the business all their working days, living above the premises. The wives from the old country often joined their husbands (some five to ten years latter) when their husbands could accumulate enough funds to send for wives and children. These children had to go to school during the day and help in the store in the evenings and on weekends. Plus there was a demand on the children to study hard to become lawyers, doctors, teachers or any other kind of professional. There was a lot of pressure to succeed placed on the offspring.

In my particular situation, my father on a trip home to Macedonia informed my mother that he was taking me back to Canada with him. I was 9 years old at the time and she begged him not to take me because

I was too young. Even my grandmother joined in the plea. I overheard this conversation, then my father informed me I was going with him to America and I was going to live with my aunt and my cousins whom I never met. I replied, "No. I don't like you." and kept my distance from him for the rest of his vacation time. On the day he was departing for Canada I ran off up our side of the mountain, fearing he would carry me off with him.

One year later, in June of 1933 my poor father sent the funds and travel documents, demanding my mother to dispatch me with haste before I got any older. I was 10 years old and he was very concerned that I would not learn the English language properly and speak with an accent for the rest of my life.

So there I was, in September 1933 enrolled in a Canadian public school, unready to face what was ahead. What a frightening shock it was. For months and months I struggled to learn enough English to be able to communicate with the teacher. I yearned for the day when the children would stop laughing at me in the school yard. My academic life I am sad to say never recovered. The subject of arithmetic gave me some hope, it being the same as Greek school classes. I was quite happy until the teacher brought down a heavy wooden ruler right across the knuckles of my writing hand that brought tears to my eyes. The reason I received this punishment? I wrote the number seven (7) the European way, with a line across the stem. The teacher did not even have the sense or the compassion to show or teach me the correct (Canadian) way to write the number. She just told me that was not the way to write a seven. That incident gave me a heavy complex. I arrived to a confirmed conclusion that I was fooling myself. I did not know arithmetic or any of the other subjects being taught in English school.

Chapter 21

MAY I DIGRESS

A constant problem is like a plague: it has a tendency to affect the entire family. The wives suffered equally since they had to put up with their husband's frustrations due to the lack of funds and yet these women could not apply for simple employment anywhere.

During that period of time (1933) my brave Aunt Keta had her family of four children and I was merely an added burden to her. My dad and his two brothers slept in shifts above the restaurant which was kept open 20 hours per day 7 days a week in the hopes of eking out an existence. They had a hard time meeting the monthly rent of 25 dollars. Their landlord was foreclosed on for non-payment of his mortgage. The Guarantee Trust Co., the mortgagor, coerced my father and his brothers to purchase the building or vacate the premises. After much trepidation, the Trentons purchased their first piece of real estate in their adopted country.

When the war commenced the economy improved and so did business. Five years later they purchased the building next door to 2570 Yonge Street, in the area referred to as North Toronto. Shortly thereafter Uncle Basil purchased the first Trenton residence on Erskine Avenue. And thus began their struggle to pay off the debts of the properties they had purchased.

Now I return to my personal tale.

We, the children, continued with school. I being strange to the language, continued to struggle with the curriculum to a point where I dreaded walking in the direction of the school. Entering my classroom was like entering a torture chamber for me. I felt as dumb as a door nail and ashamed of myself for not understanding the language. This was my third month in the country.

I picked up some profanity to protect myself from the kids who made fun of me because of my lack of English and my odd pronunciation of the few words I was familiar with. Recess period was unbearable. My back was always pressed against the school building for protection as I looked out at a sea of scrabbling, screaming little people. It was a great relief for me at the end of the school day.

I could not seek assistance from my little cousins, as they had their own friends at school to play with they were not aware of my dilemma. I kept all to myself. I could not talk to the teacher or my aunt or my father because big boys don't cry.

During this time, if you spoke with an accent or could not pronounce your words correctly, you were ostracized. Either that or they beat up on you and if you didn't fight back to show them how tough you were they would not have anything to do with you. It was the code. Hardly a good atmosphere for learning English or anything else.

I was always relieved to see the end of a school day. I waited until the schoolyard was cleared of children and then I would walk home. It was a combination of fear and a feeling I was not fit to socialize with the children. I retained this self-destructive attitude and I had never confessed my academic inability to no one until now. I classed myself as a dummy. I placed such a heavy stigma on myself and I never shook it off until many years after my school days had terminated.

Two years past. Midway through the third school year, my father and uncle decided to relocate the family closer to the newly established restaurant to cut down on street car fares and travel time. That meant, for my cousins and me, registration to a new school, which did not relieve me of any school stress.

The new school, which is still in existence today, was Eglinton P.S. located at the corner of Eglinton Ave. and Mount Pleasant Rd. I spent half a year in grade four or five because I still lacked the basics to proceed. Without the personal assistance of a tutor, which was not heard of in those days, it made it impossible to climb the academic wall and progress with the other children.

Therefore, the school in its wisdom, transferred me to John Fisher Public School which had an auxiliary class, referred to by the children as "the dumb class." My father was very disappointed. His dreams of me becoming a doctor or an engineer were dashed to pieces. I sensed his disappointment but I was helpless to do anything to correct the calamity.

I spent a year in the auxiliary class, mid-term of the second year they transferred me to a normal class in grade five. The problem was I became very self-conscious of my large physical size and this made it awful to be in class every day.

Towards the end of school term, my former auxiliary teacher Miss Donahue stopped me and asked how I was doing. I replied that the kids in my class were so small and I was so big (of course, I was normal for a child my age). I almost asked her to take me back to the auxiliary class.

A week or so later Miss Donahue summoned me to her classroom and informed me that I was going to high school with boys my own age. It was a class to prepare you to learn a trade. This confirmed my father's disappointment that I was not fit to enter the professional field. I was relieved though, since I didn't know what I was facing, to be going with boys my size and age. That afternoon they sent me to Northern Vocational Secondary School with documents for registration. I was given a class room number and reported the next day thus ending my very unproductive frustrating public school years.

The two years I spent in high school gave me some relief because I was with my counterparts but I could not break that mental academic block I was plagued with. Given my exam failures I cancelled myself out and by 1940 I was too self conscious to repeat the year.

So that summer I found a job serving hamburgers at Wasaga Beach and I tied in with another boy, Bob Brown, who would also not repeat his high school year.

It was a good summer at Wasaga Beach. The war was in its second year, and soon we would be eligible to enlist or be called up for service for King and Country. With the war planes and pilots practicing war manoeuvres along the vast Georgian Bay water beach my concern was that I did not qualify to fly, on account of my educational standing, and an eye impediment I received playing high school football. That deeply depressed me. As I watched manoeuvring practice with envy overhead, I realized that this pleasant summer was reaching a close. And I didn't have a clue about what I was going to do.

By the end of the summer, Bob bought a 1925 Chevy, on its last breath, for $21. I gave him nine dollars towards it, to complete the purchase.

The first week of September the Beach was almost empty of vacationers. Even the weather seemed to switch abruptly from summer to fall. The shooting gallery and emporium were busy with the task of closing. Our boss, Garvy, instructed us to do the same with the Hamburger Stand. He was anxious to return to his locations in the town of Meaford and Toronto. I condemned myself to return to Toronto even though there was nothing there for me except Betty McClain whom I admired and respected. I had escorted her to the show last winter. I didn't feel worthy enough because I had nothing to offer her and she was returning to school. I didn't feel her equal.

The Wasaga Beach main street retailers began boarding up the front windows. The end of the season had sadly arrived.

Chapter 22

OFF FOR ADVENTURE AND EMPLOYMENT

Bob Brown and I set our sights towards hard rock mining. Being sixteen years of age we were actually too young but we were not giving our age too much consideration, the task before us was just successfully getting to Sudbury, Ontario.

Driving off the Beach was somewhat depressing to me, but hard rock miners don't cry!

The dilapidated 1925 automobile was built boxy and high and it rattled down the highway. Heading northbound with a map in hand we were looking for side roads that could take us north. The main highway was too fast for our car, besides on smaller roads we could avoid the police road patrol. You see, our brakes were bad and the license plate required renewal. Compounding that, Bob had no driver's license and I only possessed a temporary sixty day driver's permit that was outdated.

Our first test for the car was a hill that it could not manoeuvre. After several attempts at the steep hill, we decided to conquer the incline by taking a run at it, backwards. We, very slowly, just made it to the top of the road. No wonder it was sold to us for $21. The front gears were worn out, but it did perform acceptably on a flat road. We thought the seller had given us a bargain. Ha! Thereafter, when we approached any hill on the road we drove up it backwards. Luckily, the traffic in those days was very sparse.

We spent two nights on the road sleeping in the car and we finally reached our destination, The Nicklebelt, The city of Sudbury, Ontario.

We parked the car on the outskirts of the city and slept in it that night. The next morning we purchased a little gas and used the washroom to wash up. After several attempts, we located a room and board house but we had no money for rent. We spent our total fortune purchasing the car, some food and on our travel expenses. We heard if you were looking for employment some boarding houses would extend you credit until pay day.

This was very good news for us. We checked the employment ads in the Sudbury Herald. As luck would have it there were jobs available.

We applied to a department Store called C.D.S. (Canadian Department Store) that was owned by the T. Eaton Co. On completing the application for employment, we were hired and ready to report for work in the morning.

We applied for renting a room only, requesting credit until pay day, and thereafter we planned to purchase the total package of a room with food.

Waiting for our first pay check became an ordeal due to the shortage of funds for food. We could hear the regular boarders sitting down in the dining room and the clanking of dishes and the odour of food permeating our room on the second floor played havoc with our empty stomachs.

Bob was a lot better off then I was. He worked in the fruit and vegetables department and used to visit the cellar and help himself to bananas and oranges. I was employed on the fourth floor in the furniture and kitchen flooring department. Some of the flooring for the kitchens was so delicate to handle that if you lifted the Congoleum on one corner to demonstrate it, just look out, it would tear off in your hands. Obviously you would lose a sale and the desired commission. The customer would leave the floor not bothering to look at any other merchandise in that department. Every time that happened to me, I was glad I was on a very small salary otherwise I would be working for free.

Finally pay day arrived. We were down to our last ten cents. For lunch we had purchased two bags of Planter's Peanuts, selling for five cents a bag. That evening, fortified with money, we patronized a Greek Restaurant for supper. We had passed that restaurant daily, dreaming of the sign in the front window featuring the "combination salad plate" containing assorted sliced meats with all the bread and butter you could eat. This was the first full course meal we consumed and enjoyed in three weeks.

When we settled our credit account with our landlady at 36 Cedar Street it did not leave us with too much spending money, which led us to think of hard rock mining for better pay. Unfortunately our young age was a handicap.

We had abandoned our old automobile on a side road outside of town for a while so we could get settled with jobs and a place to live and orient with our new surroundings.

Three weeks had elapsed and when we went to find, it was not there. The police had picked it up and placed it in the pawnshop. When we approached the garage they wanted more then $21, which was the total purchase price of the car. We informed the people housing our car we would return when we found the funds to bail our beautiful gem out of the pond. We waved goodbye to it through the wire fence. We never retrieved it or saw it again.

The city of Sudbury appeared like a rough-and-tumble mining town but in general the people who looked hardcore on approach were reasonable, law-abiding folks minding their own business. They were concerned about their family and hoped that their employment in mining continued.

After a payday my chum Bob and I could afford a beer in the local beverage room of the Hotel Frontenac. The place was so crowded and loud that no one asked us proof of age or anything else. Life was good.

Leaving Wasaga Beach for Sudbury, I am with pipe in face and Bob Brown, sitting on the hood of our first automobile, 1941.

Chapter 23

MORE WORK AND ADVENTURES

Going for a walk, attending the odd movie and occasionally patronizing the beverage room was all that constituted the big-time social activity of our evenings out. The little city supported one movie theatre with blazing, flicking light bulbs. It was as popular as the hotel beverage room. Walking past in the afternoon or evening the noise from that beer hall could be heard half a block on either side of its doors.

My cousin Helen and sister Christine paid us a visit one weekend during my stay in Sudbury. This was at the request of my dear, loving mother who wanted to know how her hard-rock miner son, who was employed as a clerk in a department store, was doing. Bob and I showed them the rooming house we were living in then we all had dinner in the hotel they were staying in. They left by train the next morning for home to report back to my anxious mother.

Bob also had several pleasant well-typed letters and a visitation from his half brother Bill. The Brown family had not told Bob and his sister that they were adopted and when he learned the truth it came as quite a shock to Bob and he never got over it. For that reason his school marks had taken a nose dive (he was an intelligent guy) and he also developed a dislike for all his adopted family.

In Sudbury, the two main streets were pretty active with people shopping and doing business. However there was no evidence of new houses or any form of new construction. All the buildings were left over from the long gone gold rush days. Everything looked quite worn out and contributed to an atmosphere of continuing struggle. The only reasonably new building, with stained white glass front entrance doors, was the INCO (International Nickel Mining Company) administration offices located on the outskirts of the city.

It was said that this company provided employment to eighty-five percent of the city of Sudbury and the surrounding area. Families depended entirely on this conglomerate for their livelihood. In fact the other fifteen percent of businesses existed as off-shoot of the mining industry.

We had decided that it was time we tried our luck in securing a position with this powerful company known to every person in Sudbury and district.

What did we have to lose but a potential job? Let us be turned down by the biggest in the industry, after all we migrated here for that purpose. Besides, we could not think of another place to find employment.

We approached INCO's employment office which was located back out of sight of this huge impressive structure. It appeared as an aftermath of the main construction. The small addition to the main structure did not match the building. It was attached to the ground floor corner of this huge five-floor structure, far away and out of sight of the front entrance doors.

Leading to the employment office was an unpaved muddy path with two wide planks leading to the front entrance. Inside we went down four or five muddy steps with very little appeal and which did nothing for the huge company's image. It was a small grubby atmosphere that greeted the potential employee.

From behind the teller's cage was a man with a silent look on his face that said "You'll never make it as a hard-rock miner."

He reluctantly handed us each an application form and pointed to a long grubby table with a four-inch separation wood picnic table.

After quickly putting pen to paper we handed our completed applications back to the man behind the teller's cage. He told us to sit and wait for five or ten minutes. Finally the man behind the teller's cage informed you where you were to report to or that there is nothing for you.

There was no formality or detailed instructions; just a piece of paper with your name on it and the department you were to be placed in. When you reached the mine you were supposed to hand over this little chit and then you would be put to labour.

Unfortunately my friend Bob was not hired. His height or weight had impeded him. Actually neither of us qualified for hard-rock mining, where one was supposed to earn the big dough, because of our age. I was hired but I was to report in the morning to Copper Cliff, a town that was located approximately five miles outside of Sudbury.

At 5.30 a.m. the next morning I was standing with other people waiting to board an old rackety trolley railcar that was headed to Copper Cliff. It was very dark boarding the trolley on that cold January morning to complete the "six to three o'clock" shift. I returned back with my lunch pail, my face and hands and my denim clothes (newly purchased for the occasion) covered in fine black dust. The first day had instantly immersed me as an "on-the-ground" miner, not the coveted underground miner position.

I had been hired to labour in a factory called a smelter, which was aptly named. This is where the mineral rocks are melted. They are transported in from the mines and then processed into nickel. It was hard breathing in the smelter but the work itself was not hard. I was responsible for checking the vast conveyor belts. I had to see if they were rolling and to quickly report if there were any breakdowns or falling rocks from the conveyors belt before they reached the furnaces. Should a breakdown occur, which was frequent, I was to shut off the switch and call a stand-by crew for a quick repair and I was to aid in that task. This is the way I put in a shift. I walked the two floors of moving conveyor belts watching for falling rocks and placed them back on the moving belts and I watched for any breakdowns.

It was a huge plant, with a number of overhead cranes moving this very hot liquid from one section to the other. On the way home, I could see from the trolley car the mountains upon mountains of mineral extracted rock called slag resting on the perimeter of this humongous factory.

I was receiving the great sum of fifty-five cents per hour for my service to INCO at the Copper Cliff smelter plant. The ones who made the big money were the overhead people in the cranes. They sat roasting over 500 degrees of the heat feeding crushed rock out of the deep bowels of the earth into melting pots where it was converted into liquid. They were earning, and deserving much more than, their one dollar and ten cents per hour and had to have special instructions to earn a certificate for that job. I requested crane training but I didn't have enough seniority, besides there was a waiting-line for such an opportunity.

This gives the reader some insight into the trends of that time and the scarcity of employment opportunities available to people.

While I laboured at Copper Cliffs, my friend Robert continued in the same job in the grocery store. To save money he continued his old habit of helping himself to bananas and oranges and then graduated to pilfering chocolate bars. With no first warning to "cease and desist" this practice, he was promptly dismissed for it.

My salary, combined with our meagre savings, was not enough to carry both of us and since he was unsuccessful in obtaining employment with INCO he decided to return (much to his dismay) to the family hearth in Toronto.

This slowly brought to a close our venture in the great mining city of Sudbury, Ontario. I remained an extra three months to save enough to return home not completely financially destitute.

Spring had arrived and my thoughts drifted back to Wasaga Beach where we started this venture. The working conditions in the INCO smelter were unbearable and very unhealthy for one to remain indefinitely. Wasaga Beach is where I left my youth and terminated my school-days, at the young age of sixteen. It was not the thing to do, to try and return to those jobs because they were relegated to the kids requiring summer employment and then returning to high school. I placed myself out of that category.

In retrospect, going back to Wasaga Beach for a second season to work would have been a good decision! Flipping hamburgers for a happy tourist crowd would have given me time to contemplate a new start and see where my future lay. At that time, however, I thought it was a step backwards. My pride combined with my low self-esteem would not permit it. Therefore, my life remained in limbo. I was a serious, very unhappy seventeen-year-old with nowhere to turn.

So there I was in Sudbury, without my friend Bob, and life was quite lonely. We did not have the opportunity to make new friends. We had kept to ourselves. We went to the movies and went out for the odd beer at a crowded beverage room in the local Frontanac Hotel. My last evening in Sudbury was spent with a lady in a room above the beverage room; very enjoyable indeed. She was couple of years older then I and very desirous to leave Sudbury, which I was doing that morning via the train. I had to make haste and return to the boarding house to grab my belongings and be at the station to board the rail car bound for Toronto and my family.

I can't say I was sad to leave that industrious city of Sudbury and the soot that floated from the smelter. It laid all over the walls of all buildings, the sidewalks, the streets and the faces of the people coming off their eight hours shifts from the smelter. I was still spewing it out for the following ten months after leaving Sudbury.

Of course you cannot produce 95% of the nickel in the world, at that time, and not show evidence of it on the labouring population. The people labouring in the task to process the nickel did not show any particular discontentment on their faces. It was something they were compelled to do to maintain their family. They had no other employment choice but labour in the mining industry.

I said a silent adieu and felt no nostalgia for Sudbury as I waited to board the train bound for Toronto. And yet I faced a bleak and uncertain future before me that concerned and depressed me to my very core. Everybody heads to Toronto for employment opportunities. I being so ill equipped for any type of employment could not see the vast choice of industries to seek employment.

After a six or seven hour train ride, I disembarked at Toronto's Union Station.

I was not particularly happy to be back. I felt like a failure and not just because there was no one to meet me at the station.

I boarded the streetcar directly north on Yonge Street where my family resided over the restaurant. Nothing had changed in my last ten months of absence. I was facing that bleak and uncertain future.

Reaching home, once the greeting and hugging by my dear mother was over with, I tucked the whole experience of the past ten months away in my mind and never spoke of it. The only reminder I had of the north country was that spewing and coughing out the soot our of my lungs for months later.

At this time, the war was well on its way. The ammunition factories were humming and the recruiting posters were in evidence to encourage you to do your duty and enlist to serve your country. I did not attempt to seek employment to earn a better then average pay because I felt they would not hire me as I would soon be conscripted into military service. So I continued to work in the restaurant for my room and board. I, being not quite military age to enlist, did very little to prepare myself for it. When the day arrived to put on a uniform it was somewhat of a shock and a complete change of lifestyle.

Chapter 24

THE ROYAL CANADIAN MOUNTED POLICE

My first attempt to enter into the military was with a great desire and enthusiasm.

Influenced by my exposure to the movie that was popular in those days and had impressed me deeply, was Jeanette MacDonald the opera singer and her boyfriend Nelson Eddy in "The North West Mounted Police". In the movie they sang a variety of songs. He, on a horse and she, in open horse and buggy, crooned away with such songs as "Rose Marie I Love You "and "The Donkey Serenade." They influenced me to the point of providing me a great desire to join the great The Royal Canadian Mounted Police.

While working for my dad at nights in the restaurant for my keep (no pay) during the day I filled out the endless paperwork and obtained character references from adult individuals who knew me. I needed to obtain papers from my church and submit to physical examinations for entrance into the great RCMP. I was getting ready to don the uniform and board a train west to the province of Alberta and the Mountie Training Academy. We were told at the recruiting office that when you had completed and passed the many tests you would be posted in the wilds of Canada or anywhere you were ordered to do go. Oh, what sweet sound.

One evening, while waiting to hear the results of our physical and written tests, I started talking to a young guy I met in the recruiting office. We were walking along the boardwalk on the popular Sunnyside Beach in Toronto. We were revelling in our thoughts of joining the Mounties and as we passed by one of the hamburger restaurants we spotted the Mountie who had interviewed us for the Force. He was with his girlfriend so, with a little trepidation, we went into the open-air restaurant, approached his table, excused ourselves for interrupting and stood at attention like good Mounties should.

We asked him how our allocation was coming along and how soon we would hear the news, "Sir-ring" him with every sentence. Of course the young Mountie was impressed because his girlfriend was. This was our purpose, to help him impress his girlfriend, so he could help us to pass our written test.

The young Mountie was pleased with our approach and inquiry. He replied "You fellows should be on your way to Calgary. You'll be notified to report for duty in a few days."

We walked away floating on air all evening long.

As the Mountie predicted that evening at Sunnyside, about two weeks later I was told to report to Front Street, the Mounties Toronto headquarters, to hear the results of our test and physical.

To my surprise I was turned down! I did not qualify for the Royal Canadian Mounted Police force. I was not born in Canada and only British subjects or Canadian born were permitted entrance into the elite Northwest Mounted Police force. What a huge disappointment and a shock. I was not worthy to wear the uniform of this elite special force. I felt like a second class citizen. I did have one small consolation. I had feared I could not pass the written test, which by the way I never was given nor was I given the results of my physical.

I expended about five months in this futile exercise in my attempt to enlist in the Mounties. I was now close to eighteen years of age and the conscription age at that time was nineteen so I felt I better make haste and choose where I wished to serve my country before they make a choice for me.

Two months later, walking into the Canadian Air Force Recruitment Centre on Bay Street in Toronto, my mind was definitely made up. If I was to die for my adopted country, I would do it my way! Filling the application for service, I stated "pilot" and no other choice out of the list of 1) Pilot, 2) Navigator, 3) Air, or 4) Gunner. I stumbled through the written and other tests as best as I could and I was instructed to report for a physical test a few days later. Then you were kept waiting for a few more weeks before you were given the results. I was called for a second eye test and then told to wait several more weeks.

Finally I was called to be issued an air force uniform. I was taken in with a few others and was informed I did not qualify for pilot air crew because the sight in my left eye was not 20/20, much to my surprise and shock. The reason I was called in for a second test was to confirm this impediment in the left eye. It had been injured, not seriously but enough to stop me from flying an airplane. It was then I recalled my last year in high school playing football. In a practice game I had scored a goal and the team jumped all over me with joy while I landed in the cinders on the running track. My eye was sore for weeks thereafter and my dear mother begged me to quit playing football.

So I replied to the Air Force interviewer that I would be happy to be a navigator and he replied that I didn't qualify. I still needed good eyesight to be a navigator. There was a lot of night flying, "Okay," I said to him "I'll take air gunner."

"There is a high casualty rate for air gunners. You need excellent vision for that job. We can't fit you into an air crew. Will you join the ground crew?"

I replied, "I'll think about it."

With great disappointment I left and never returned to give him my answer. I did not want to go ground crew, while people I knew made it into air crew. At that time that thought was very disturbing to me. I had failed for the second time to attain my desired goal. It brought my morale down bellow ground-crawl level.

Then a thought came to mind, "Am I fit to enlist in any branch of the military? Mentally or physically?"

To think of enlisting in the Navy is out of the question! The freezing cold deep blue Atlantic Ocean, was most unappealing so I scrubbed Navy service out of my mind. Besides, the bell bottom trousers were unappealing to me personally. I had several friends say they would take no other military service because their fathers served in the Navy. My father had served in the Army. I wondered if a son follows his father.

I would have considered the Navy Fleet Air Division but because of my experience with trying to enlist in the R.C.A.F., that thought was impossible to contemplate. I got the courage to try the Air Force exam because a school chum whom I thought was less competent then I was had made it into a pilot training program. This had given me the courage to try the Air Force.

When I had attempted to enlist in the Navy Fleet Air arm they would not even permit me to enter the front door of the recruiting centre. Only high school or university grads would be considered. This thought had prevented me from attempting to enlist. I defeated myself before trying.

The Fleet Air arm had enviable smart looking white uniforms with brass buttons and a cap with a spread eagle attached over the peak. It was the most appealing of all the military service uniforms.

My mind was scraping the bottom of the barrel that I found myself in. My lack of formal education prevented me from reaching or attempting to try for anything that I truly desired with pride. I had already attempted many things without success. A very disheartening and demoralizing experience! I had reached a new low point in my life. I was wondering whether I could even pass the Army physical test due to my six months employment in the INCO smelters in Sudbury? I was still spitting out black soot.

Reaching the bottom of my life's totem pole affected my lifestyle and my presentation in trying to put my best foot forward in written test and interviews. It was particularly depressing to me as I worked the night shift in my father's restaurant in order to have the days free for interviews and to assess my situation while I played a little pool.

My father's restaurant was a sort of meeting place for young people in limbo, who were attempting to enlist in the military. Hearing them boasting, discussing and exchanging ideas and desires for the military choices depressed me deeply, I felt I was a most unworthy waiter with my white apron, serving fountain Coca-Cola, coffee, grilled cheese and western sandwiches, which were popular in those days.

After brooding for a while, with much trepidation, I approached the Army Recruiting Centre for Toronto on Albert Street. It was located on the second floor with no one in evidence outside of the building to encourage you to join the Army. Ascending the worn wooding stairs up second floor you were met with a large area full of young recruits sitting on long benches around the wall of this huge room. The centre of the area was also occupied with benched and long tables and full of people busy filling out application forms.

The uniformed man with stripes on his sleeves sat behind the wicket. With no formality or questions asked he handed me an application form and a test paper saying. "Look it over, and when a seat is available take it, sit down and fill it out."

One sheet of paper was your identification: your name, address, phone number, next of kin, in case of an accident whom to notify, etc. The other sheet was a test, first asking how much education you had and then proceeding with a common sense questions such as, does the sun rise from the east or the west? If the sun was setting in the west which way would your shadow fall? Also there were some simple arithmetic questions plus some no and yes questions that filled up both sides of a large sheet of paper.

After completing this test I was told to go into the next room and wait for the M.O. (Medical Officer) for physical inspection.

The doctor arrived and seemed in a hurry. With the aid of a Sergeant in uniform he tested us six to ten at one time. We were lined up in a row and he ordered us to strip down to our underwear. Then told us to stand on one leg for a few seconds and then on the other leg. He looked up our buns with a flash light, checked our eyes with a chart on the wall, looked in our mouth and ears and asked if anyone had a disease. I would say the physical took less than twenty minutes for the ten recruits.

They sent me home to wait to be called. Two weeks later, I was advised to report to the Exhibition Grounds to get measured up for my uniform. They came in small, medium and large. The shoes the Army assigned you were made with a little more care. They had a solder measure the length and width. He was very accurate in new his job, I have never had better fitting or more comfortable shoes, which I found out was very important in the Army.

Then they sent us home and ordered us to report back in ten days. Upon reaching home, I walked into the restaurant and the first words my father greeted me with were, "You are going to get killed in the uniform!" The ten days quickly passed.

Chapter 25

YOU'RE IN THE ARMY NOW

I reported to the Horse Palace at the Exhibition Grounds where instantly the aroma of horse manure was heavily prevalent. I never got used to the odour that would assault me every time I walked in from the outside. After all the horse resided there many years before man took over the premises for the duration of the war. How long that would be, man did not know.

300 to 400 bunks were assembled for sleeping on both floors of the Horse Palace. It served as a holding unit to accommodate the new recruits before they were shipped out to the various basic training camps.

The horses were not as crowded as we were. I wondered if the horses were as uncomfortable with the human's odour, as we were with theirs. This was my introduction in to the Canadian Army.

Drilling commenced right away. Right turn, left turn and walking was no longer permitted. Everything was on the double. We were issued rifles, with no bullets, for drill purposes on the asphalt parade square. The Drill Sergeant would blare out with "You may have broken your mother's heart, but you are not going to break mine!"

A couple of days later I was ordered to report on the double to the Catering Officer, who held the rank of a Major. In civilian life he was the General Manager of the Royal York Hotel (now the Fairmont chain of hotels in Canada).

Standing at attention in front of him, he was sitting behind a desk. He informed me, with the first civil voice by a military person of any rank since my induction into the Army, "I am looking for recruits. I notice in your file you have a restaurant background. You can transfer with me. I am starting a food training program to teach cooking and food training. And when you're finished, you'll be sent on an Officer's course, if you qualify. Then we'll send you out where you'll be inspecting kitchens and mess halls in Army camps. Think about it, Private, and let me know before you are shipped to basic training camp."

I was then dismissed. I saluted, and left his office.

Not having made a decision yet, the company I was attached to was informed of a ten mile route march, to New Toronto and back. An hour before leaving I was ordered to report to Major McKinnon, the officer who interviewed me a couple of days ago. He asked me, "What have you decided? If you join me you don't have to go on the route march. I'll train you in the food service business and after the war I'll place you in one of the Royal York Hotels and train you for a manager's position."

I replied, "Sir, I had enough of the food business. I am not taking up that career after the war."

"Okay," he replied with disappointment. "But because you're physically fit there is no other place in the army for you but the infantry!"

Declining an opportunity of that nature with so much potential when re-entering civilian life was folly.

The only comment I truly heard the Major say was I was "physically fit", like he had bestowed on me a badge of honour. Happy on the route marching through Sunnyside, I was thinking my health had survived the smelter of Copper Cliff in Sudbury.

Turning down that Major was a major mistake. It was the only opportunity that was rendered me in the Army. No promotions came my way. There were people with over three years of seniority waiting in the Army for advancement.

While at the Exhibition Grounds waiting to be designated to a camp, I was compelled along with the rest of the Army personnel (about 200 men), to witness a disgraced military discharge. He was a North American Indian who was convicted of stealing, rape and other charges. This individual was already convicted and had served time in a military prison. It was quite a dramatic procedure. He was brought in chains, escorted by the military police, and paraded in front of the total military camp personnel.

The regimental Sergeant Major read out loudly the numerous charges he had served incarcerated. He was found guilty of stealing, rape, drunk and disorderly contact, etc.

The Sergeant Major blared out a statement, which was very effective "You are not fit to wear the uniform of a Canadian army soldier!"

Then a Sergeant and a Corporal proceeded to cut and tear off all insignia and gold buttons from his tunic and wedge cap, converting his appearance to that of a drunken bum.

The last act of this ceremony saw the accused escorted by the 200 witnessing soldiers to the Princes Gates. He was instructed to never go near a military base of any kind on threat of a further jail term without a trial. The chains and hand cuffs were removed and he was virtually kicked out on his ass with those heavy army boots. He shuffled his way up the street, while the witnesses watched him disappear, in the sad remains of his uniform with buttons torn off and lapels flapping. It was a sad sight to watch.

This rare ceremony was to serve as a warning to the 200 witnesses to behave and "toe the line".

The next day was Friday and we were scheduled for a fifteen mile route march, which was cancelled and we were given the weekend off. We were then told that come Monday, we were ordered to bring all military-issued paraphernalia packed in our kit bag and leave all civilian clothing at home. We were leaving for basic training camp.

The military mandated that we were not allowed to give information on troop movements. It was always a secret, so we could not divulge the information to anyone, not even our next of kin.

It is beginning to feel and smell like a place where no one wanted to be. But there was no way out. You're in the Army now, Private. Unless you wished to go the way of the court marshal we had witnessed the other day.

Come Monday morning, a roll call and check of all the names was made, just like in a chain gang in the movies. The troop train arrived in the Exhibition Grounds and after another roll call was made we boarded. With four soldiers in each car and the very last person to board, the Provost Corporal, we were finally off. The train chugged slowly along the train tracks, past Sunnyside Beach Park where just a few months back I was seeking information from that Mountie with his girlfriend, regarding my entrance into the Royal Canadian Mounted Police. It was sad that it was all history now. I sat wondering when I would return to walk in the Sunnyside Amusement Park again. I was sad and homesick and so soon.

It was still a secret mission with some guy saying we were heading for Brantford. Two and a half hours later, with duffel bags in hand, we disembarked at a train station. Parallel to the train, we could see the huge military transport trucks that we were to board.

Other trucks rumbled in front of the train station where there was the sign in green lettering: "Brantford Station" with one guy yelling welcome to Brantford. This was my first visit to this town. It was December 8, 1942 and the camp was located east, just on the outskirts of the town. I was to train for the next three months.

I completed advanced military training, Camp Borden Unit, Ontario, 1943. On draft for England and further training for invasion into Normandy, France, 1943.

I am in the basic training camp, Brantford, Ontario, 1943.

Chapter 26

BASIC ARMY TRAINING CAMP

On arrival to Camp, we all lined up on the parade square that we were going to see a lot of over the next few months.

First the Commanding Officer gave us an introduction, then the Padre spoke and finally we were handed over to the Regimental Sergeant Major for other brief talk. We were told that reverie was at 600 hours sharp and henceforth that was the way you would express the time. Breakfast was at 700 hours. If you missed it you did without. Parade was at 800 hours. Then Dress for Inspection and on and on. All expressed by the hundreds.

We were assigned a billet that reminded me of a giant garbage can cut down the middle and placed upside down on the ground. But it was an improvement from the Horse Palace at the Canadian National Exhibition grounds. It was all strange being in these new surroundings.

A tremendous amount of snow fell that winter. Just my normal luck to receive my basic training in the middle of winter in 1942/43. During the Christmas holidays we received an extra couple of days leave and free train transportation home.

On our second interview with the Army, they asked us where we would like to serve in the Army. I requested Paratroop training in Fort Benning, Georgia in the USA. This was where all Canadian Paratroop training took place since the Canadian Army did not have Paratroop facilities in Canada.

I heard rumours that the Army was constructing a Camp in one of the western provinces for such training activity but my preference was Fort Benning.

They placed my request in my file and I never heard any more of it until my basic training was completed and I was ready to move out with the rest of the trainees to an Advanced Training Camp. I was called in and advised that the Paratroop Training facility in Fort Benning, Georgia was no longer available to the Canadian Army and the facility in Western Canada had not been completed as yet. I would have to request a transfer once I received and completed the advanced training.

On completion of advanced training, on the last parade I was ordered to advance in front of the Commanding Officer. Like a properly trained soldier, I came to attention and marched in a square in front of the Commanding Officer.

He advised me that the paratroop facility was still not completed and I would be on the draft for overseas. However I could apply for paratroop training overseas. Then he barked, "Dismissed."

I, saying not a word, saluted, and returned to my place in line with very great disappointment. The thought that came to mind was, "God, I can't even choose how I was going to die for my country."

Another desire dead.

I was so very disappointed. I was looking forward to earning a wing on my uniform. Luck was not in my corner. Being turned down for the Paratroop Regiment I felt justified to protest and to go AWOL. (absent with out leave). But then I thought of my family being in the restaurant business. When our customers heard about me "taking off," my family would be disgraced, so that idea was dismissed from my mind.

Returning to my quarters I prepared to go on leave for our last weekend. Another soldier who had also applied for paratroop training was advised he was to be shipped on draft overseas, was almost crying. We became buddies and ended up in the same regiment (The Royal Regiment of Canada) overseas. Peter Walsh and I kept in touch with each other until his death in 2004.

During this time, we began our heavy training schedule with route marches in the winter blizzards, training on the parade square with the winter winds and drifting snow viciously blowing across the Camp grounds while you took your turn on guard duty. Duty was of course on a 24 hour basis with stocking the stove being an all-night ritual. For the designated soldier there was hell to pay if he fell asleep and forgot to feed the stove with coal.

We trained with World War One rifles that had been moth-balled in some military storage area for over twenty years. It was surprising how well-persevered they were.

The extreme vicious winter days were reserved for lectures, map reading, gas mask handling procedures. Our evenings were occupied with preparation for the next day; cleaning your boots, checking your uniform, showering and tacking your shift at stocking the stove in the nesting hut.

Some of us would slip into the town of Brantford for a couple of hours. We left that mostly for weekends, when we could take in a dance sponsored by the Red Cross, or have a beer in a beverage room. We were safe as long as we returned to camp before bed-check. At one of these dances I met a young lady with olive skin, dark jet hair and eyes to match. I think she may have been Armenian. She let me walk her home and we promised to see each other in the near future. Before reaching her house she told me that we'd better say goodbye there. Her father and mother were home waiting for her. We exchanged kisses and then reaching a modest street with attached housing, we talked briefly in front of her house and made arrangements to meet next week at the Dance Hall. I don't recall seeing her again but we wrote each other a couple of times thereafter.

However on my way to Camp that evening I was approached by a man and asked if I wanted to have sex with the lady who was seated in the window. There was no charge for this as she was just feeling hot that night. The time was approximately 10.30 p.m. and I got very suspicious. We had been lectured on sexual diseases such as gonorrhoea, the clap and syphilis and this had put the fear of God in us.

I replied "No thanks. Maybe tomorrow. I don't have time right now. I have to get back to Camp before eleven hundred hours".

And I marched off quickly.

The very next day, they had the whole camp on the parade square. The Sergeant Major announced that there had been a rape in town committed by a solder. The mother and her daughter were in the Colonel's office and they were scheduled to come out and the rape victim (the daughter) would identify the guilty party.

The Camp Commander appeared with the mother and the daughter, who had tears in her eyes. The party was escorted by the Sergeant Major and they commenced walking up and down the many columns of soldiers. They would pause and look at the faces of the soldiers. This took close to an hour with no results. We all watched the Colonel escorting the mother and the daughter to the gate of the camp as they paused for a while before departing.

Even those of us who were innocent breathed a sign of relief to see this parade terminate.

The parade was dismissed with the Sergeant Major barking, "Return to your duties."

We kidded each other saying things like "They missed this time. "They will get you the next time."

On a serious note though, the Camp's permanent personnel, including the Camp Commander, rendered us tremendous protection by giving us advice regarding scheming women that made a career marrying a soldier as many times as they could. These women had hopes of these poor soldiers going in to battle and being killed in action so that they could collect a widow's pension.

One way the Camp rendered us protection was if a woman accused a soldier of raping her they would have us line up to be inspected by the injured party. If you were wearing your uniform that evening, you were ordered to change in to your fatigues (working clothes) and visa versa. The woman would have to recognize you not your rank or uniform. That was part and parcel of a life in the military.

We completed basic training by mid March 1943. At that time a local farm boy in our age group was absolved from further military training due to the employment he had was necessary to the war effort. I remember the day we shipped out for Advance Training Camp. He turned in his uniform to the quartermaster and came back to the hut in his civilian clothing and yelled out us, "So long, suckers!" His name was Bartozic.

Hearing him blare out like that I had my mixed emotions overpower me. I silently called him a coward and then praised him for finding a way NOT to die for his country. Oh how I envied him.

So there I was after three months of basic training being herded onto a troop train. We were not aware of our destination, of course. We had all seen the promotional materials, Billboards were everywhere with statements such as "LOOSE LIPS SINK SHIPS" and "HITLER HAS BIG EARS".

Chapter 27

CAMP BORDEN FOR ADVANCE TRAINING

The troop train stopped at a small town called Alliston, Ontario, that is located just a few miles south of Barrie. As per the last move, a convoy of military transport trucks awaited us parallel to the train tracks. We disembarked and then embarked onto the trucks in orderly fashion like mature soldiers; after all we just completed basic training which placed us in an advanced category.

Camp Borden was perhaps ten fold larger compared to Camp Brantford both in military population and land mass area. It housed most units of the Army components plus an Air Training Facility with air landing strip. Every division was doing their own business and not particularly paying attention to what the other units were doing. Therefore my draft contingent arrived unnoticed and commenced to merge with other incoming graduates of the basic training course from other Camps. Constituting a full Regiment of 565 personnel, all of us were classified as "general service". This meant you would be placed anywhere the Army needed you to fill a void. The infantry was to be placed in Regiments overseas and they were to give priority to individuals requesting a specific regiment.

I did not have a regiment choice. And I knew nothing of the history of any of them. I purchased a Toronto Scottish wedge cap at the basic training camp in Brampton because I liked the colour and it fit my head. The Toronto Scottish Regiment was a machine gun support regiment, which would have suited me quite well because this meant that there were not so many route marches. However, once we got overseas to England it was a war zone with bombing almost daily. This led me to have second thoughts about joining a Scottish regiment. I was not even of Scottish descent and if I got killed overseas in a Scottish regiment and all my records destroyed, (communications not being what they were then) I thought, "I am not of Scottish descent. They would go to Scotland looking for my kin folks, without success!"

I would therefore be listed as are many "as the unknown soldier". That thought did not appeal to me. Therefore, reaching overseas, I didn't choose the regiment. When I was asked, returning from the company headquarters, I requested be placed in a Toronto non-nationalist regiment. I must have made that statement to some fellow soldier(s) and perhaps leaving my Scottish wedge cap exposed out of my kit bag, I discovered it missing, I hope the person who permanently borrowed my wedge cap was successful in getting in the Scottish, and survived the war.

The other reason I chose to stay out of the Toronto Scottish Regiment was because of a fellow by the name of Jack Mitchell. He was an older guy who had hung around my father's restaurant and he had joined the Scottish regiment. He would call me, a Macedonian, a fraud and besides he did not like me. I am puzzled to this day why this person intimidated me. I did not admire him or particularly dislike him, he was just a customer in the restaurant, and we could use as many of those as we could attract.

Thinking back I guess it may have been an incident that occurred back when I was waiting to be called into the army. We were both past high school age but Jack Mitchell had asked me to go to a football game with him. At the time he was only actually interested in a cheerleader at a football game but he convinced me to go with him to the game. At the time I was kind of impressed that he would ask me to show him where the match was being played. We boarded a streetcar together but upon arriving at the stadium he told me to "beat it", in a way that conveyed that he didn't want to be seen with me and that I would spoil his style. He hurt my feelings. I thought he accepted me as his buddy. So, I went my way and he went his, and he didn't get the girl. She smartly kept company with a guy her age group.

I digressed, but I thought I should clarify how an incident that concluded months or years after was important to me at a particular juncture in my life.

Back to CAMP BORDEN... and commencing advanced training. We were no longer called cadets. We were soldiers. And we were to walk and act like one at all times. The advanced training was much the same as our other training with route marches, parades and drill work. Plus we now had the added rifle practice and grenade tossing, field work and the fun of crossing bridges and water with a full sixty pound equipment on your back. Extreme safety was emphasized in the handling of weapons. Rifles, pistols, hand grenades and Bren guns (machine gun). A number of accidents were caused in training by mishandling weapons. There was also more emphasis on gas masks. We learned about the care of these units plus the ability to use a special chamber to sample the smell and taste of the gas for a few minutes, for the sake of recognition.

On night patrol, some guys had commercialism in their soul. They would pack chocolate bars and sell them at a profit on route marches.

It is no wonder that one was not able to develop any close friendships. You were kept too busy at all times throughout your basic and advanced training. We hardly knew anyone. We only knew each other by our last names that we would find out by hearing the Sergeant yelling at us, always during morning roll call. You would come to attention and you would answer "Sir. Trenton B-136570."

When you would receive a weekend pass, you'd leave and return on your own. You'd walk in a group or with a buddy then board a bus or a train to your destination. We would all go our separate ways, anxious to see kin or friends and receive a release from the army life for a while. Very few familiar faces of the young people I had known were available when I reached home. They had been seconded into one or the other military services. Thereafter, our lives were changed permanently as did the atmosphere on our section of Yonge Street. The poolroom and my father's restaurant had lost their glamour for all those young men lucky enough to survive the war.

It made me wonder how many of us were going to make it out of the military alive.

On leave, I had the phone numbers of several girl acquaintances. If one was not available another one always was. I had taken one girlfriend for a ride in my father's first (second-hand) automobile, a 1936 Ford. We parked on the side of a road, presently the sight of Sunnybrook Hospital) that was unpaved. The wheels sunk up to the axle above the tires. We tried to get out but only succeeded in digging us in further, right into the soft earth and melting snow.

After an hour or so we realized all this effort was futile and I had to catch a train for the Camp. We left the automobile stuck in the mud and snow and started walking with frustration and at a fast pace. I was thinking about what I was going to say to my father. What to do? What to do? I walked my girlfriend to her door and ran like hell home to our apartment above the restaurant. I grabbed my kit bag and the rest of my gear and ran downstairs. In the restaurant my poor Dad was dumbstruck. He didn't know what hit him. I told him that the car was stuck in the mud and needed a tow truck. I felt badly because my poor Dad didn't need that extra expense. I gave him directions where to find the auto then I put the car keys on the cash register. Not waiting for his response I told him I must get back to Camp and left. I climbed the streetcar with great relief and headed for Union Station. On arrival, the station was saturated with military personnel. We were all heading back.

On my last leave before shipping out overseas, I made contact with a girl I met at Wasaga Beach. Betty Bettis and I went dancing at the Pallas Royal in Sunnyside. During this time we made a few commitments to each other to write. And she gave me an address to look up her uncle who was living in London, England. Betty even attended my bon voyage party before leaving for overseas that was arranged by my sister and my cousin Helen.

This last leave also gave me some time to re-think the idea of going AWOL (absent without leave) in protest to the Army for declining me paratroop training at Fort Benning, Georgia. In retrospect I should have made that decision and disappeared for a few weeks (I would have missed the draft) and then return back to Camp in two or three weeks. Then again that re-occurring thought of disgracing my family, and jeopardizing the restaurant business that my father and his brothers struggled to keep afloat plus missing the draft for overseas constituted desertion, which meant a court marshal, I didn't know whether that constituted years served in prison or being shot. This was what we were led to believe in those days, when your country is in state of war and under marshal law. Even if I were to disregard all of the above, I didn't have enough self-conviction to take a runner for the north woods.

While it was difficult to develop close friendships at this time, we were comrades in arms and were developing a regimental "esprit de corp". We were learning to automatically depend on one another to do our share in the field of battle. It is a somewhat different camaraderie to a friendship where one confides his dreams and aspirations. The tone of this friendship never changed, except in my situation. At the end of the war my buddy, of the few that were left, struggling with their wounds and physical deformities, looked me up. He had known my father had a restaurant on Yonge Street called Trenton Grill. We were true friends. Along with our constantly training, we would gather at the same pubs to drink luke-warm beer. We competed for the same girls at the same dance halls in England. And on French soil where we were wounded, although at separate times, we ended up in the same military hospital for Canadians in England. This friend was Peter Walsh.

My buddy Peter even had two cousins living in London close to the Canadian military hospital. In fact, they came several times to visit us by our bedside. If we were fit to be placed in a wheelchair the two girls would roll us around the hospital corridors. This made the situation a little more bearable while we were waiting to be shipped home in a hospital ship.

Chapter 28

ON DRAFT FOR OVERSEAS

By April 1943 advanced training was completed. Those who could not take the riggers of the infantry, or had special skills, were designated accordingly. Most could not escape the infantry, due to a big demand for it in the Army.

As previously mention in these pages, I was informed for the second time that there would be no paratroop training for me in Canada. Try again, overseas. Thereafter I tolerated the army because I was compelled to do so and I tried to make the best out of an inescapable dilemma.

Packing personal army gear and appearing on the parade square for the farewell speeches of the top army brass, including travelling rules and regulations, the conduct of a soldier overseas, occupied most of the warm sunny morning.

The next morning boarding the troop train leaving Camp Borden, we felt like a herd of cattle boarding. As we were viewed by the permanent training staff I heard one say, we were heading for slaughter. My feeling was synonymous.

The saturated troop train was slowly heading south through Toronto. We made a stop on the bridge over the liquor store at Summerhill. Just below, we were over-looking Yonge Street, my street, with my father's restaurant located only four miles north.

Oh how I wished I could see him going in to the liquor store below to pick up his weekly supply but no such luck! At this time he would be busy preparing the noon hour lunch and thereafter he would be cleaning up, without my help. Then he would take the street car to pick up his weekly supply but that would be around 4.00 p.m. He would then hurry back to prepare for the supper period. I knew his schedule. I had often had to mind the store in his absence. Gosh I became so homesick! I didn't know when or if I was coming back.

My parents knew that last weekend was my last one before I was to be shipped overseas. But they did not know when and neither did I.

All troop non-events were top secret. Remember LOOSE LIPS SINK SHIPS. It was mandatory and vital but oh so hard on the soldier and his kin.

It was a twenty minute stop, just enough time for the locomotive to fill up on water. No one was permitted to get on or off this over-saturated troop train. Then the train chugged along out of the beautiful city of Toronto and I wondered when or if ever will I see it again.

We were heading to the east coast, Halifax, which was the only disembarkation point Canada had in those days. We stopped in the province of Quebec for more water for the locomotive and box lunches were passed around to all. We then moved on the tracks leading into the U.S. and stopped somewhere in Vermont.

The security seamed to have eased off over the border. Vendors at the station were selling fruit and sandwiches. They handed them up by reaching up to the windows of the train. Some soldiers sneaked off the train and purchased a case of American beer and it loaded onto the train. It was a warm sunny spring afternoon and we seemed to have paused for a while longer compared to previous three Canadian stops on the route.

The mobile troop contingent moved on down the track, eventually reaching its destination of Halifax, Nova Scotia. The total train rolled into a covered barn structure that swallowed all the cars. It stopped along a huge wooden platform the size of a football field. On the other end of this platform was the ship waiting for us to board with four or five loading planks leading onto the huge monster floating on water.

We disembarked the troop train and began assembling equipment, etc. and with a lot of shouting by NCO's we lined up. I was amazed how many the troop train carried. I guessed the count over a regiment was close to 800 military personnel. I was wondering if the ship could accommodate us all.

As we boarded the ship in an orderly manner, much to our surprise there were 2,300 military personnel already on board waiting for us. We were the last contingent to arrive. Some soldiers had been on board ship two days. Now I knew how sardines feel in a sealed can.

The ship pulled up anchor as soon as we boarded, heading out in to the dark gray sea.

We were escorted by five smaller fast ships, two leading and three following, plus two submarines on each side of the ship. All out of sight.

The boffer guns onboard ship were manned 24 hours a day. The ship was manned by the British Navy, with the merchant marines employed as labourers.

Teaching us the use of the English money that we were to use henceforth in England was important. As a teaching instrument the British sailors used a pair of dice, which was most profitable for them, and a fast way for us to familiarize us with the pound, shilling, crown and tuppence, the basis of English money.

The name of the ship was the "Empress of Britain" the same ship I sailed on at the age of ten to migrate to Canada from my Macedonia in northern Greece. The ship had seconded and converted to a troop ship shortly after commencement of the Second World War. My gosh, it never occurred to me while crossing the Atlantic ocean for the second time my father was not invoiced for this trip. This time the passage was for free except that my family paid with stress, concern and worry.

The ship must have been loaded from the top down since we were allotted sleeping quarters so far down in to the bowels of the ship. Each corner of the cargo area had a layer of ice a foot thick. We slept on tables and hammocks hanging over the tables. This served a dual purpose as they were converted in to dining room tables for lunch periods. If the ship was torpedoed, this area was submerged under water, as it would have been hit first and instantly filled with ice cold Atlantic sea water.

It required seven or eight flight of stairs to reach the first deck to see the light of day and fresh air. This was distinctly different from my tourist class travel on my first ocean voyage on this ship.

On board ship, after one dispensed with his English money on the dice table, there was not much to do on this six day ocean crossing but walk the very congested deck looking out in to the grey, heaving ocean water. Talking to other Soldiers from other parts of Canada, and finding why they had joined the Army I found most of the answers to be, "I was going to get drafted anyway."

Other soldiers who were recent arrivals (one to five years) to Canada from Great Britain, said they were asked before leaving the British Isles if they would come back to defend England in case of war. Other young men had recently married their sweethearts, just days before being drafted for overseas. This group was so homesick and just anxious to get the war over with. I doubt if there was a human being onboard that ship that was not homesick and concerned for his well being. Would he survive the war? I fell in to that category.

Approaching the British Isles from a distance, we could view the huge balloons appearing like zeppelins tied up over land and over cities for protection from enemy aircraft. One of the newly married soldiers was so depressed and homesick, he remarked, "Let's cut those balloons down and let the Island sink and turn this ship around and go home."

Chapter 29

ARRIVING IN ENGLAND

Hours before sighting land, it was blared out over the loud speaker we were arriving to safe land. We finally reached and sailed up the English Channel docking at Plymouth. It was a foggy dull afternoon and the docks were busy with weary exhausted people loading and unloading precious goods for England in order to survive and not particularly paying any attention to this huge monster of a ship disgorging thousands of military personnel.

The familiar military truck transport met us there for boarding. In some strange way the procedure gave me some comfort to "soldier" on. The military transport trucks were the only sign of "Welcome to Britain".

With haste the truck convoy went rumbling down the winding roads of England. We were happy to disembark from the huge floating steel monster ship that gave us a hint of war and some fear of enemy torpedoes.

Overhearing one of those sailors after a week's leave say we are heading out again and we don't know where (not even the Captain is aware until he opens his sealed orders) until we are out to sea is not a very pleasant life for a sailor. Mobile on the road, yelling over the noise of truck engine, exchanging comments, and curious as to where we were heading, someone yelled "Aldershot" which was the holding centre for the Canadian Army and a distribution centre to units and regiments that are in need of reinforcements. Sure enough we approached the outskirts of a fare-sized town called Aldershot. It was an old military town occupied by the permanent army before the First World War and a good majority of the houses was tenanted by army families.

The convoy entered a mud/stone wall fence that exposed an area that would occupy a football field if it had not been for the soldiers living quarters, drill field, headquarters and lecture rooms.

We disembarked in a unceremonious manner, with the regimental Sergeant barking out orders to everyone on staff and we were assigned to our sleeping quarters, and then he ordered us to grab our mess tins and report, as he pointed to the Mess Hall.

As one walks through life, as I have in this book, I have attempted to use the vernacular, but eliminating the generous use of profanity, of that particular time.

After supper we were free for the evening to roam around the town. The barracks were located almost at the centre of Aldershot. Most of the pubs were filled with noisy military personal, who had walked further, reaching the outskirts of the town. It was in one of those pubs where I had my first order of the famous English fish and chips, although you were to call them chips and fish. Wrapped in real newspaper, the grease was never changed and it was obvious food was rationed because the grease stuck to the roof of your mouth. This was the first time I realized the true application of rationing. These people had no alternative choice but to persevere through the many hardships of war.

The next morning we were awakened at 06.00 hours but it was no hardship for I was used to it and it seemed so were the rest of the new arrivals to Britain. After breakfast we were all lined up on the parade square. It was very foggy morning and we could not see the either side of the field. The Regimental Sergeant Major barked out orders trying to straighten out this and that. All of a sudden, we could hear a voice from a distance barking out orders to the assembled troops.

The Regimental Sergeant Major came to attention and made an about-turn with his back to us, yelling out, "Colonel Christie, when I am ready to run over the parade to you, I will let you know, SIR!"

Then the Commander of the Aldershot camp replied, "Sorry, Sergeant Major. Carry on."

The Regimental Sergeant Major saluted the Colonel, about turned and faced the men and continued barking orders. I and the rest of the soldiers were shocked and impressed at the same time. Not everybody can get away with yelling to a Colonel and Commander of the camp like that. In war or in peace time. I thought to myself if I take up the Army as a career, I would work myself up to a Regimental Sergeant Major, and emulate this man.

That evening, I visited the Canadian Army Community Room in town where they supplied you with blue writing paper with a stamp attached. I was anxious to write home to the family to tell them that I was in England (Of course I was not permitted to say exactly where.) I wrote my letter and handed to someone to censor it and then they mailed it for you.

On my way, I bumped into Tom Simon, a young man who was my age. I had known him and his family ever since I arrived to Canada from Macedonia. My brief conversation with Tommy revealed he was as concerned and homesick as I was and he was shipping out in the morning. Bound for Italy, he thought. I never saw Tom again until we all came home. He died early in life though he survived the war. He passed away in his fifties.

The following morning we were ordered into the orderly room and were told where and approximately when we were to ship out. I was ordered with a few others in the infantry regiment. The transport number was 55. When that numbered truck arrived in camp I was told be on it. That Regiment was my permanent attachment henceforth.

Chapter 30

THE ROYAL REGIMENT OF CANADA

A period of five or six days had elapsed, when the transport # 55 with the red and white maple leaf had arrived to pick up approximately twelve of us to a place not known to us and an infantry regiment with it's origins in Toronto that was completely unknown to me and I suspect a stranger to almost all the soldiers assembled with me ready to board as ordered on truck # 55 belonging to the Royal Regiment of Canada.

While waiting our time was pretty well our own. Some were in the recreation hall playing pool or kicking a ball around. I attended an aircraft recognition film, distinguishing between allied aircraft and enemy planes. While listening to this lecture and viewing the various type of aircraft, a loud blare came through the loud speaker, "Attention. #55 transport has arrived. All boarding it, pick up your kit bags and all your personal belongings and report in front of the orderly room immediately!"

Where was it taking us? The location of course was not revealed.

We left Aldershot, on #55 with a feeling of never returning to it again.

For the last six months I had been shunted here and there, back and forth, hurry up and wait. A nomad does not move so often. Not without choice, at least. It was a very demoralizing and depressing feeling, I must say.

The transport was heading for the south coast of England, where all the Canadian Army was posted to guard the south coast of Britain. Not known to us which was north, south, or what have you made the situation more devastating. I felt like an expendable commodity led to slaughter.

A lapsed time of three or four hours driving around windy single lane/double roads through towns and little hamlets until we finally arrived in a forest nowhere near the sea view. It was called the Goodwin Forest, re-named by the soldiers Sherwood Forest, and it was located on the side of the hill under huge trees accommodating assembled tents as sleeping quarters. The lowest, most distressing situation so far was that the cook house, a Nissen Hut, with its the familiar tin garbage can cut in half, length -wise, had smoke pouring out of it while the other half of the garbage can served as the men's Mess Hall. On the other side of the cook house were the tents occupied by the Officers with the Padre's tent in front. A wood board attached to the tent indicated the tenant. Across the road on a flat area was the parade square. In war time, to write a letter home describing the above, was tantamount to two year in a military prison.

The dreary dismal English damp weather made the situation worse, but here we were.

The Army, I had discovered had an answer, a procedure or a rule for every situation a military personnel encounters, whatever it may be. There were Part One Standing Orders; which covered everything a soldier encounters; a crime he may commit, or an honour he may deserve, how to conduct himself on leave, when he eats and when he sleeps. Then there were Part Two Orders, covering the daily routine, who is on duty, who goes on leave his destination and when he is due to return, and if he commits AWOL (absent with out leave) what punishment he would receive.

It was here in Goodwin Forest that I learned about the Royal Regiment of Canada. It was an offshoot of the Royal Grenadier Guards with its origins in England. They were originally stationed in Toronto serving in Canada during the North West rebellion, in the Louis Real period. During the 1930's and 40's almost all the Officers in the Royals were employed in the stock market or the Bell Telephone Co. in Toronto. They joined the militia as a hobby or form of recreation, previous to the war breaking out and had received their Commission through that channel. I wished I had had the foresight to join some military unit for a little experience, and then I would not be presently serving as a lowly, expendable private.

When I was fifteen years old I asked my father if I could join the Governor General's Horse Guards. They rode real horses and I was excited with it all! They had very smart uniforms with shinny silver brass head gear with a streak of high bristles on top. They were used in ceremonies by the Governor of Ontario. But, my father being a six-year veteran in the Greek Army in the First World War and the Turkish Rebellion, gave me a definite NO!

"I don't want you involved in any kind of military affairs, keep away from them", he ordered. "Besides I need you to work in the restaurant."

He and his partner brothers did have a hard time making ends meet in the restaurant business.

Back to the Royal Regiment of Canada. Henceforth, as they called the regiment, I shall refer to it as the "Royals".

The closest to a decent-sized town was ten miles from Camp. It was called Chichester and each evening a transport truck was available to anyone wishing to spend the evening in town. Pick up was eleven hundred hour. Visiting the city of Chichester was alright as long as you did not consume too much beer and lose track of the time and miss the transport truck back to the Camp which many did. It was a long walk back to Camp in the dark since no lights were permitted in the outdoor on any night.

The Army was not noted for hospitality. The Padre (Minister) was available anytime but we would try not to disturb him. He would be around the camp or the mess hall if you wished to talk to him.

Colonel Nicholls was the Commanding Officer of the regiment and he spoke to us two days after we arrived in the presence of the total Regiment. He sounded like a visitor to the Regiment, which he was. A few weeks later his transfer came through. He shipped out to take charge of another regiment that were fighting in Italy, where the war was in full bloom. When I heard this I was reminded that my cousin Alex Trenton was over there with a Tank Regiment. I wondered if we would meet.

The Colonel leaving us was an executive with the Bell Telephone Co. in Toronto. He was instrumental in recruiting a lot of employees of Bell into the peace-time militia I mentioned. And, at the end of the war, when he returned to his civilian position with the Bell Telephone Co. he gave preference to, and hired many veterans serving with the Royals. When I returned home from the war, the thought entered my mind to go to him for a job but my bum leg was a detriment as I was unable to climb telephone polls and those were the jobs that paid the better money in that business.

Bivouacking in on the side of the hill in Goodwin Forest outside of

Chichester we began training for a mock war, coordinating with the total 2nd Division of fifteen thousand men, which included the Royals Infantry of Toronto, the R.H.L.I. of Hamilton Infantry, and the Essex Scottish Infantry of London, Ontario, and the Toronto Scottish Machine Gun Support Regiment. These units composed The 4th Canadian Infantry Field Brigade.

It all became clear to us new Royal recruits that the training and coordinating for war was called the "Spartan" exercise scheme. The Spartan exercise was particularly important because the upper echelon was assessing the Officer's leadership abilities as well as the men. Some coordinating route marching was involved on manoeuvres with the 2nd Division. This served to clarify confusion in a real battle. Thereafter arrived a report with some praise and much more criticism of the Officer's leadership.

There were many schemes of this nature in smaller proportions on the Regimental scale and Brigade competitions kept us so involved in preparing for battle that we had little personal time. Now I think the training saved a lot of lives.

Chapter 31

DEAN PARK – HORSHAM

The Spartan scheme was over and we, the new inductees to the Royals, survived it with no regrets by any of us and we had successfully blended in with the rest of the soldiers. It was time to pull up the tent pegs, which we were happy to do.

In an orderly fashion we embarked onto those troop transports with the maple leaf with the number 55 on each front and rear fender. Rumbling down the road we headed to Dean Park, which I and the other new arrivals have never seen. It was in West Sussex, England. Dean Park was on a flat hill located above the large Town of Horsham.

The huge building was on the park which was 600 years old. It had had many owners; the most recent occupant had converted it into a school house before the government seconded it for the Army shortly after commencement of the war. The structure served as the Regimental headquarters, and the Officer's Mess and recreation hall, with the Colonel's and the Officers' sleeping quarters on the upper floor.

Surrounding this building were indiscriminately placed Nissen huts that housed the mess hall, and also the four Company Orderly rooms and the rest with sleeping quarters. The parade square was located in front of the castle-like structure and utilized for almost every activity in the military outdoor lecture parade plus lots of drill work and personal recreational sports.

A typical military home, the confinement barracks (jail house) with its seven-foot high narrow windows to deprive the occupant a view to the outside world, overlooked the huge parade square.

The area occupied approximately a one mile square and was enclosed by a twelve-foot fence that was constructed many years ago of rock and mud. Military police guards occupied the front iron gates.

The city of Horsham was medium-sized, and friendly and tolerant of the military much the same as other towns and cities.

The pub owners all over England were the only people thriving as well as the owners of the breweries processing this malt in their factories. Every commodity was short and rationed except the luke-warm

Beer. Refrigeration in all the pubs in the country was non-existent. The cold damp cellars where the barrels of beer were stored and pumped up to fill the drinking glasses was the best they could do to cool the beer. However, I never heard anyone including the American soldiers complain about the temperature of the abundantly available beer in England. Perhaps beer served the war effort as a morale booster to the military personnel.

Chapter 32

TROOPING THE COLOURS

Here is a brief history of the Trooping the Colours. All Infantry Regiments in the British Army carry their own personal battle flag which is given to them by the person holding highest title in the land. This emblem is carried by the battalion into battle. Should the situation become critical, before they engage in the battle, the flag is buried and a map is drawn up of the location which is known to one Officer, one Non-Commissioned Officer and one Private only. At the end of the battle or when the survivor(s) return they dig up the flag and return it to the Regimental Headquarters.

In the Dieppe raid of August 1942, The Royals suffered 90% casualties therefore the battle flag was lost. The infantry Regiment cannot go into battle without a flag. They must comply with tradition and replace the lost battle flag.

It was August 1943 and The Regimental Sergeant Major called out the total battalion out onto the parade square and announced that they were going to pick 110 of us to attend a flag course. Ten of us would fail. Two officers with the Sergeant Major commenced walking up and down the straight-as-die lines pointing at a soldier and barking at him to step forward. It must be said that the infantry could never win a diplomacy contest. I was one of those soldiers chosen for this two weeks course.

Next morning we boarded those Number 55 troop transports and off we went, rolling down the English roads, while no one had been told our destination. Two or three hours later, we disembarked on a University Campus. Our equipment was unloaded on a smooth asphalt-covered field that we would be seeing a lot more of. We were billeted in the school dormitories and on the same day we arrived we were introduced to four Scottish Guards, each one over six feet tall, who were going to be our drill instructors.

After a decent night's sleep, the Scottish Drill Sergeant commenced the course by saying, "I know you have done a lot of parade square drill work. Well, I want you to forget everything you were taught. We are going to start new. My way."

We commenced with left turn, right turn. It was August, sunny and hot on that smooth drill square. Some soldiers fainted while others were found with unclean rifles and such and were disqualified for it. By the end of the two weeks of gruelling drill we were ready for the big parade. Our backs were as straight as a ramrod. There was just one problem. There were two too many soldiers. Only 100 were required, not 102. The Colonel asked for two volunteers to step out of the Parade but no one volunteered. The Colonel then offered a week's leave. Still no one volunteered. The ones he picked at random were disappointed and ready to cry.

Finally came the day that we had all laboured for on the drill square. We were assembled in a straight line of 100 of us with ten Officers on each end. Arriving on time were Their Majesties, the King and Queen of England with their daughters Princess Elizabeth (our present Queen) and her sister. The King's entourage was simple, containing two limousines. One carried the Royal family, with two motorcycle escorts. The other containing military staff was bringing up the rear.

The Royal family were first to step out of the automobile. They were greeted with salutes by the waiting military staff on hand while the parade was brought to attention as the band played the national anthem. At the same time the Princesses wearing duplicate blue-valved coats were escorted to a viewing stand especially constructed for the occasion. The King was escorted with top brass to proceed with the inspection of the troops. The Queen followed with her escorts. The Royal couple on their inspection tour periodically would pause and ask a soldier what part of Canada they were from, or ask if the soldier was home sick. At the end of the inspection His Majesty placed a new battle flag on the holster of a kneeling soldier who was waiting for it. Thereafter photographs were taken with the King and Queen then the Royal family had lunch with the Officers.

The soldiers had lunch and following a old tradition, Beer, compliments of His Majesty.

I prolong this tale because it was the highlight of my army life. I was so overtaken with the royal family and their effort towards the war effort. When he was asked to leave England for his and his family safety, the King declined.

Life in the military, especially in the infamous infantry, was a series of constantly playing war games. We witnessed the demonstration of a weapon that would not destroy a tank but immobilize it, if you made contact with the track of the tank or had a direct hit on the weakest part of the steel monster. It looked like a large kid's toy and it was just as dangerous. The demonstration proved its effectiveness was nil. It did not have the power to reach the target but bounced thirty feet from the shooter and hopped like a bunny twice on the ground before it came to a halt. With the rumbling of the invasion into Europe that spring, this demonstration was very demoralizing indeed. To think of relying on a pea shooter to stop an on-coming enemy tank.

We had target practice, but only five rounds per man, as we were rationed to save the ammunition for the real thing, it was said. Route marches were always available when nothing else was and also the gas drill and demonstrations into gas chambers to feel the effects and to test your equipment.

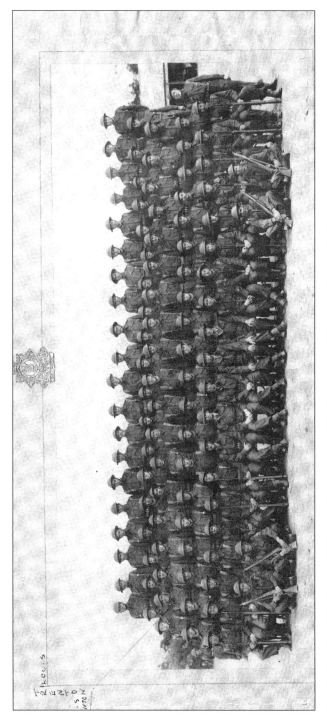

No. 6, The Royal Regiment of Canada, Presentation of Colours by the King and Queen, 1943.

Chapter 33

THE TRENT RIVER CROSSING

It came time for another scheme at the town of Scunthorpe, where it was close-by the wide Trent River. This was to familiarize us with dis-embarkation and embarkations from a small landing craft, by jumping into the water close to the shore in full gear with out rifles and machine guns to be kept dry. We experienced a few broken limbs, in that week's stay on the outskirts of Scunthorpe, where we spent our evenings in this busy little city, with plenty of pubs and lots of competition for girls from American soldiers.

We received a lecture from our Regimental Padre Appleyard. He was mad as hell because of the atrocious and loud use of profanity we indulged in. His lecture lasted about 20 minutes. Padre Appleyard was with the regiment from start to finish. He followed the battalion almost to the front line with his reverse white collar around his neck and red cross on his sleeve. He visited the wounded back in the field dressing station, he administered to the killed and removed one portion of the dead soldiers dog tag and recorded the soldiers' names.

After the war Padre Appleyard attended each November the 11th at the survivors annual dinner. He would bring his record book and read at random a dozen names. All the men had a soft spot for Padre Appleyard. He became a bishop of the Anglican Diocese, plus the honour received from our government. All the men respected him.

Early New Years Day 1944 the Royals were inspected by the C.O. (commanding officer) of our division who was the blue patch Second Div. Gen. Charles Foulkes and then later in January by the Corps. CO Gen. G.G. Simonds.

On March 21, 1944 we were inspected by Gen. Sir B. L. Montgomery. The location was on a cricket field on University grounds. We were lined up straight as ramrods, all spit and polish. The General walked through the front rank of each only of the 4th Infantry Brigade. Then a well-polished Jeep appeared and drove to the middle of the crick-et field, then the short, little General walked over to the shinny Jeep and a wood platform was instantly placed on one side, startling the front and the back seat rests. The General stepped up and onto this wide flat sturdy wood platform. He ordered the huge, perfectly formed lines of military precision to break rank and gather around him and the glossy Jeep.

In his made-to-measure special-material battledress, adorned with First and Second World War medals he proceeded with his speech to this vast assembly of military personnel. (I quote in part from memory.) "You will have a blanket of air power over you, which will, in advance, destroy everything before you. The Navy is trained and well-armed to convoy you there safely."

He verbally painted a picture of the invasion. All the Infantry was left to do on the French beach was to take out our mess tins and have a picnic. He wished us all well then departed, with his royal entourage.

I was not convinced by the General's speech. Perhaps I was influenced by a comment I heard or read that the Queen was bestowing a Lordship on him and invited Montgomery's mother to the affair, He had replied, "If that woman attends, I will not!"

I wrote Montgomery completely off my personal "like" list when we were fighting and dying in France, and he was conducting and directing the English and Canadian Army from five miles back of the front line. Gen. Montgomery awoke one morning from his comfortable caravan, looked at the map, and said "What are the Canadians doing back there? They should be here!" and issued orders immediately without investigating the problem of the situation. His order to push forward created a tremendous amount of deaths and wounded young men (of which I was one of the wounded).

The rumour was Montgomery was in competition with Gen. Patton of the U.S. Army to see who was going to reach Berlin first.

On March 9, 1944 we were inspected by King George VI. We assembled on both sides of a rail road track and stretched for more than two miles with military personnel, including the Air Force and the Navy. His Majesty, on approaching, saluted every Regiment. By the time he past the Royals he was fagged out, with a pale appearance. He was not a well nor a young man, for this type of a performance duty.

The above inspections were followed by more playing war. We called those schemes: "push" "night" and "step".

In April the Royals moved under canvas (bivouacked) in the marshalling area of a town called Betteshanger. Living under the air route that was used nightly by German Bombers to reach their target of London, we were to attempt to shoot them down.

During the same period of time we had our little home-spun drama. The performance of two Ojibwa soldiers mates which resulted in a fatal argument over a sandwich in the Mess Hall.

One final exercise before real action was the four week scheme "kate" with assault boats in waist-deep mud of the Trent River.

The next VIP inspection was by the US Gen Dwight D. Eisenhower who visited the 4th Infantry Field Brigade. I can not recall any portion of his speech.

Late May of 1944 was a very tense time for England especially the mass allied military force waiting for the proper weather conditions to cross over to France (not known exactly where) to commence the beginning of the end of the War that has entered its fifth year.

While we awaited the order for the Invasion, the Germans had invented what we named "Buzz Bombs" launching them from the coast of France and sending them gurgling their way lazily overhead, seeking their target the City of London. The first launch of this deadly rocket bomb was in daylight but they flew slow enough so that we could shoot them while airborne and minimize casualties.

The Germans via their spy net work became aware and changed tactics. They began dispatching the deadly Buzz Bombs at night, therefore making it too difficult for us to bring down or explode them in the air.

Chapter 34

INVASION INTO NORMANDY, FRANCE

Preparing for the Invasion, we had to turn in our uniforms and fatigues for one uniform that had been deloused and a new gas mask that was checked that it was in proper working order. When turning in my uniform I neglected to remove my good luck charm given to me by Barba Thanasi, a chef who worked for my Dad in the restaurant, that was pinned to my inside pocket of my tunic. I remember when he called me to the kitchen and handed me a piece of folded cloth, two by two inches and one-quarter inch in thickness, and said these words, "Do not open it. This will save you. Keep it with you except when you go out to do bad things."

I replied, "Okay, Dedo. (grandfather)." And he pinned it on the inside of my tunic pocket.

Now I had left it in my tunic in with a mountain of uniforms. I was frantic. I approached the Quarter Master, to plead my case. "WHAT." He bellowed.

After a while he said, "If you can find your tunic," as he pointed to hug pile of neatly tide tunics, "go ahead, but you will put them back the way you found them!"

An hour or so later, I breathed a sigh of relief as I pinned that piece of cloth with the original pin that the cook had given. What a kind but lonely old man. He had adopted us as his family and we called him Barba (grandfather) Thanasi. God rest his soul. He passed away before I left for overseas.

The cook, Barba Thanasi, lived in the Turkish era and he had to migrate out of Greece. He was a big man physically and he had had a confrontation, with a Turk. There was a scuffle and the Turk was killed. The Turkish authorities had a head bond on him and he ended up in the deep forest in the United States, cooking in a lumber camp. Many years later he migrated to Canada.

Before leaving this camp in south England, several of us drew midnight watch which was spread over the Camp. We were to be on the alert for the "Buzz Bombs" sputtering over the Camp on their way to drop on the city of London. While on night watch, walking to investigate some-thing, I entered another guard's territory. The soldier yelled out, "Who goes there?"

I recognized his voice so I replied, "Just me."

"That is not proper identification!"

He raised his rifle, and just about shot me down! We were all pret-ty high-strung about the forthcoming Invasion to be announced any day now.

It was finally time to move.

We pulled up tents and moved to a humongous embarkation centre on the seashore for our mandatory forty-eight hours stay (security rea-sons?).

These huge three or four barns structures housed the American, English and Canadian Armies ready for crossing. We were all enter-tained in one to the barns by an American orchestra popular in those days. They entertained us with great desire and effort and the huge Barn was so packed with soldiers sitting on the rafters clapping and shouting. The musicians combined with the soldiers were trying to cheer up the situation, desperately trying to drive out of our minds what danger faced us. Emotions ran high and were revealed on the face of every soldier all around. They were concerned, scared but no one verbalized this in case demoralization set in. So we held it in, steadfast.

The next VIP to pay us homage was Winston Churchill, the Prime Minister and War Lord of England. It was the day prior to our departure for the Invasion into France. We loaded into medium sized crafts by Company of units, (feeling quite snug) ready for action. It was a late, sunny afternoon as we were embarking the sea craft. Over the loud-speakers all around ship, announcing our attention, and introducing: "The Prime Minister, Winston Churchill."

Speaking over a cracked gramophone turntable on a 78, that had developed a crack that could be heard with every rotation of this many times played recording the contents of the speech that included segments of wishing us well and God's blessing. He wished he could join us. He said "I asked the King's permission to come with you but the King declined and said my age will not permit the riggers of battle." He then wished us all well again, and God's speedy return.

It was a long wait on board ship. We sailed for Normandy France at midnight to enable us to hit the beach under the cover of the night. About 5 miles before the beach landing, we switched and boarded five LCD (Landing Craft Departure) by individual companies who had months of training together. It was mandatory we fight together.

My regiment, the Royals, was the seventh wave to land, which was having great difficulty winding around sunken small and large ships and landing crafts. The dead, limp bodies of the soldiers were bobbing up and down in the water, some face down surrounded with their own blood. Arms and legs floating aimlessly in dark, muddy, mad seawater, and the waves, unconcerned by it all, were busy driving furiously onto the Normandy Beach.

This was an instant reality into war.

Strategically speaking, launching and landing an attack in the location chosen for the Canadians to fight on was, and should have been, questioned by our higher command. We sailed into a horseshoe-shaped beach, with high ground on each side. We attracted fire from three sides. The direct front could not be avoided. The two sides of the U-shape created a pincher exposure. We were floating ducks, front and two sides and this created much more casualties then necessary. A straight, wide frontal attack would have resulted in fewer casualties.

No words were spoken amongst us, but I, like the others, was glad that the Royals were not the chosen Regiment to hit the beach first. It was a slow approach but as soon as the landing craft touched the rock and sand bottom, the steel door dropped forward into the water. We stormed out, as though we were on a training exercise, with our rifles high to avoid contact with the water thus putting the weapon out of commission.

There was no enemy on the beach, on either side of the U-shaped trap we sailed into. The first assault regiments paid the price. The evidence was on the water and on the rocky beach of dead mutilated bodies.

The fighting was about a quarter of a mile ahead. We could hear the artillery fire. We walked across the beach to a road where we boarded transport trucks that were waiting to take us on the five minute drive to the frontline. One soldier blared out "Is this trip necessary?"

It lighted the gloom and doom for the moment. It was quote constantly seen on billboards everywhere in Canada and England for the purpose of conserving gas. "Is this trip necessary?"

We disembarked the transports a couple of hundred yards from the front line. The Royals relieved the Glasgow Highlanders from Scotland or at least what was left of them. The location was around a hamlet called Eterville but this ground was not fully occupied by just the Glasgow Highlanders, the German patrol was prevalent. There was sporadic fire around and at us, it was active but out of sight. Classified, so far, as no man's land, in a light forest area of Normandy.

My first close up of a dead soldier was in this area. I slipped out of my slit trench, for something, and I became trapped in a barrage of enemy artillery. I dived for shelter beside a trunk of tree when the firing temporarily stopped. On the other side of the tree was a guy sleeping under his ground sheet, undisturbed by it all. I approached him and nudged him with my boot to his on the ground, and said to him, "Hey, didn't you hear that?"

Then I noticed he was wearing the Glasgow Highlander insignia on his tunic sleeve. He was dead and somebody had thrown his ground sheet over him.

There was enemy sneaking around in and out of this area with the odd rifle fire. They were holding their ground undermanned and when the enemy observed reinforcements, they retreated.

On the other side, our Quarter Master was stationed a quarter mile back from the battlefield. It was his job to supply the truck with ammunition and food rations, etc. The noise back there was too loud for him so he went AWOL (absent with out leave). He was found wandering the shore of the French beach, the last we heard of him.

The quantity and quality of the equipment in the Canadian Army for the front line soldier was sadly neglected with no thought given to the effectiveness of the weapons provided for him and therefore no security to enter the battlefield. Whatever equipment we had we were undersupplied. We were told they were saving the good stuff for the real thing in the field of battle. Be it reinforcements, rations (food) or ammunition they were always coming but they never did.

Chapter 35

THE BIG BARN ON THE EDGE OF A LITTLE HAMLET

I recall, it was approximately our third week of fighting in Normandy, France and forging ahead was to say the least a struggle.

It was late afternoon and we took refuge in a wheat field and dug in for the night. The enemy spotted us from their hilltop location. Any movement in the wheat by us was death by their sharpshooters plus bombarding the wheat field with their artillery at us all night meant we suffered a great amount of casualties. Out of twenty-seven men in my platoon, there were eighteen survivors, making us the largest platoon in Regiment. We had a saying in the battlefield that "every night dig deep, it maybe your grave".

The platoon was divided in half, nine men each and we commenced receiving instruction from the two surviving Lieutenants of my "C" company, when they were called back to Brigade Headquarters for further instructions. The two Lieutenants on returning to our platoon received a direct hit to their jeep and were killed instantly. The Company Commander informed the Sergeant Major of the tragic incident and then ordered the Sergeant Major to take charge of what was left of the Platoon. We could hear him yelling at the company commander, "You should not have sent them, Sir. You should not have sent them, Sir."

The efficient Sergeant Major had instantly taken charge of the nine men waiting and started moving towards our target, the one side of a huge barn structure. He then stopped and ran across towards my section (a 100 foot distance) with a machine gun in hand, and blared out at me, "What the f--- are your waiting for, Trenton? I'm not doing this alone! Get going!"

I moved my nine men section to the south end of this massive barn. We had good coverage, a thick forest with tall trees with a creek running down the centre of the forest.

The Sergeant Major's nine man section was not as lucky, as they were exposed. It was higher ground, a ploughed field with very little cover. They were also disadvantaged by a huge opening on their side of the barn, exposing them to enemy fire. There was no such opening on our side of the barn.

The brave Sergeant Major with his nine men held their ground. The merciless enemy machine gun and the sharpshooters' fire power were too much. They were all killed, unknown to us.

Throughout the night long we returned enemy fire. We had to be careful, we didn't run out of ammunition because there was no sign of it coming or food or reinforcements, as promised. We held our ground, sporadically returning fire.

When morning came we were left with no fire power to take over the barn so we waited for the reinforcements and supplies, with no sign of them arriving. At dusk, about 5.00 p.m., the enemy shooting ceased from the barn. We assumed and readied for their attack. We were doomed since we had no ammunition left, just the hand grenades; one in hand and three each in our pouches. Hand grenades are very ineffective unless your enemy approaches within twenty feet. Then, if you don't have immediate cover, the spray from the grenade becomes as dangerous to you as your enemy.

With great relief we viewed in the early dawn of day a small patrol of reinforcements approaching cautiously in a line on each side of the open field, towards us. We prepared to clear the barn and the large house in the other side of the barn. The Lieutenant in charge of the relief patrol handed us a Bren gun (machine gun) and ammunition and ordered us to cover them while they cleared the barn.

A while later the Officer yelled from on top of the barn ordering my squad to start clearing the house. With much grumbling, since we still had had no food or rest, we commenced towards a large homestead. As we approached this elaborate farm home, a French civilian appeared and excitedly ran toward us with his hands up in the air waving and yelling, "Anglais! Anglais! You saved my town. Merci! I shall report you to Paris!"

One man in my section walked over to the little, portly French man, saying to him in a belligerent voice, "We, no Anglais. No Anglais. We are Canadiese! Canadiese!"

I said to him we have to go through his house to make sure there were no German solders. He replied "No Germans. They left."

We got suspicions at his remark and ordered him to march in front of us as we entered the house. With grenades in hand we had him go first into every room and the basement of this huge house which was full of office desks with German swastikas on the first and second floors.

Later, we were informed this was the German General's Headquarters, which was responsible for the defence of the entire French sea coast.

We also discovered the squad on the other side of the huge barn all killed; one by one by the rifles of German sharpshooters.

We never used the term "he was killed" or "died of wounds" and no elaboration. If one was sure his buddy was killed, he would say: "He bought it" or "He went west" and drop the subject and never speak of him again.

There were many instances my regiment, The Royals, faced danger almost nightly against the famous German General, Kurt Myers and his Panzer division, this was just one tale. Long after the war, my regiment selected four veterans, at random, to receive the French Foreign Legion of Honour, bestowed on us from the French government, for services rendered. I was one of them. I feel that the Sergeant Major's squad was the one that should have been awarded the French Foreign Legion of Honour, in place of my squad.

Back to battle…

Thereafter the new reinforcements carried forward to the ridge ahead, to the night, while my squad was ordered back for a three-hour afternoon relief, which was very welcomed. We then moved up to the ridge ahead to join the new recruits, who were recently off the boat from Canada to make up a full platoon. Later that night, the company was brought up to strength which rendered some confidence to move forward into the German line.

Approximately two weeks had past with a repeat of the above and each experience was a little more stressful than ones previously described. We continued digging our graves (fox holes) in pairs of two or individually, sleeping in the sitting position. We never (seldom) dug trenches long enough for one or two soldiers to stretch out. We dug the trench just deep enough to render protection form flying enemy shrapnel and bullets. At the end of the day at the form line we were too overcome by fatigue and stress to dig an inch lower then necessary. Besides that it was a waste of energy and time because you could be ordered to move forward on a moments notice. We dug trenches with a miniature shovel that was strapped on each soldier web belt. This little instrument after use, gave the infantry soldier much security.

Speaking from personal experience:

WAR IS NOT, as it is depicted in the movies, with a crescendo of a sixty-piece orchestra in the background, while the box office hero is dodging bullets and his machine gun blasting the bad guys.

There are no such thoughts in a soldier's mind as standing up tall for love and glory of your country and your burning patriotism or 'I'll show them I am a hero'.

The facts are, when necessary, which was often, you crawl on the ground; conceal yourself behind any object for protection because you don't want to die for any cause. In a heavy bombardment you frantically dig like a mole a shallow grave not to die. Self-preservation is the ultimate motive. To survive, nothing else matters. A soldier's bravery on the front line is hidden so deep into the soul, it does not exist.

The soldier who receives a medal for bravery over and beyond the call of duty on the front line is so overcome with fear of dying that his mind becomes distorted and he performs foolish acts.

The next day (as usual) we did not know what was facing us.

Covering the area allotted to us, the Regiment was moving forward in crooked line in an open, huge field. On a high ridge the enemy waited until we advanced midway in the exposed grassy area, in full morning sunshine. The enemy opened up a full barrage of fire power at our tanks leading us up the high ridge. The enemy fire power was so severe, they demobilized the two tanks leading us (there should have been five tanks) and the one armoured car was stopped to play dead. One tank that was rendered out of commission was turning in a circle on one track and smoking.

The white hot flying shrapnel from the enemy's anti-tank guns did my Company a great deal of damage (again) leaving the infantry soldier to draw his last breath and many of us wounded (I being one of them) and forcing the Regiment to retreat to fight another day, without me!

One of my buddies violated the rule and stopped beside me lying in agony. He removed my first aid pad from inside of the netting of my steel helmet, and applied it to my stomach to stop the bleeding, remarking, "Jesus Christ, Trenton!"

Then he yelled stretcher bearer and I told him to carry on, which he did and he dropped thirty yards ahead of me. I raised my good hand to get his attention but there was no answer. His body laid there motionless. His name was Nick Nicholls and he was from Manitoulin Island, Northern Ontario. He had come to Toronto looking for employment, finding none he joined the army. We did Basic and Advanced Training together and we were on the same draft for overseas. I do hope that God saw fit to bless his short live on earth.

An hour or so later, one of our jeeps approached me lying in the field. He was our stretcher bearer with a Red Cross bag over his shoulders and a white cloth with a red cross attached to the jeep. His buddy assisting him was killed.

The first thing he did was administer morphine to kill my pain. He said, "Don't worry, I am taking you back to the First Aid Station where they will fix you all up."

His name was Corporal Smithy. His uniform and face was bloodied. He was exhausted but not quitting.

On the way to the First Aid Station, I passed out. When I woke up, I was amongst rows of wounded, waiting their turn, on the operating table. A Chaplin leaned over me with a container of rum. He asked, "Soldier, do you have s stomach wound?"

I whispered yes.

He replied, "I am sorry, a drink would do you more harm." and walked to the next wounded patient, repeating the same question.

The Canadian First Aid Field Dressing Unit had very concerned and capable personnel rushing about trying to treat all the wounded, at one time. And there were so many wounded and bleeding. The young doctors and interns fresh out of schools from Canada were being ordered about by older physicians, and the nurses being worked to exhaustion.

While waiting for my turn on the operation table, I was given more morphine. I do not remember being carried into the surgery room, which was actually a tent. When I awoke it was the middle of the night. There was a white sheet over my face. As I attempted to remove the sheet with my uninjured hand, I could hear the patient on the next bed, yelling in English with a German accent. "Nurse, Nurse, he is alive. He is alive!"

A nurse, followed by a medical officer came to my attendance. With a surprised look, (they were ready to bury me in the morning), the first thing the doctor said to me, "You're going home to Canada, son. Your injuries are quite extensive, but we will look after you. You will be okay."

He uttered those words with his face almost touching the side of my face.

A couple of days later, the surgeon that performed the operation on me, Dr. Spahn, paid me a visit, and said, "We removed most of the shrapnel from your stomach. We wired your ribs together and installed a "colostomy" which you will be using to eliminate your bowel movements for three or four months. It will be closed up when you get home to Canada. You will be receiving a daily dose of Penicillin to prevent disease. It is the latest discovery and it works wonders on most people. Let's hope it does you some good."

The next I heard of Dr. Spahn he had become Chief of Surgery at the Hospital for Sick Children on College Street in Toronto. I was driving by the hospital and I thought of the Doctor Spahn. I parked my car and entered, requesting and interview with Dr. Spahn to thank him for his service rendered.

The Man was in conference, as I explained my reason to the receptionist, she suggested paging him out of his meeting, for a minute. I replied no, I would wait. An hour elapsed and I left the hospital to my regret to this day, without thanking the good Dr. Spahn.

And now I resume my life's tale...

A peculiar situation or was it fate, regarding the patient in the next bed to me who spoke English with a German accent and yelled out in the middle of the night, "Nurse, Nurse, he is alive. He is alive!"

A day before the enemy killed or wounded all of my Company (myself included) and most of my Regiment in that wide-open field a strange thing happened. It was dusk and the bombardment from the enemy was harsh and concentrated on us. We received orders where to take refuge in a wheat field. We dug in and avoided movement of the wheat to avoid attracting enemy fire.

From their high ground, the enemy spotted us in the wheat field and buried many of us in our dug up slit trenches.

A stray enemy shell hit the side of a barn on my side of the wheat field. Out came a German soldier with his hands up high in the air, his body glued against the wall of the barn. "Well," I thought, "If I die in this wheat field, you're coming with me!"

He was thirty or forty yards away and I raised my rifle and aimed at the unarmed German soldier, directed my rifle sight right on his forehead. A few minutes passed. I could not pull the trigger on him! He was mesmerized and helpless. I well remember that German soldier's face, hatless and blond hair. He was the one lying in the next bed to me, who yelled. "He is alive!" while the medical staff had given me up for dead and was scheduled to bury me in the morning. Was this incident luck? Or was it a coincidence? Or fate?

My stay in the field hospital was a few extra days. My life still hung on a balance each hour of the day since I had lost much blood and my bodyweight was down to 95 lbs. My hair rubbed off on the pillow sheet until I was almost bald on the back of my head. My weak thoughts turned to my dear mother and how it was going to affect her if I expired and that I'd never see my sister's newborn child, and my father's remarks when he first saw me in uniform, "You will get killed in that uniform" and how our restaurant chef we called grandfather had tears in his eyes on my last weekend home.

Laying down all day, trying to gain enough strength to be transported out, day and night we could hear the frontline bombardment from both sides. I was so weak I was reaching such a low point in my tender thin life that my mind was hallucinating. A voice was saying, "Who wants to live in a world, a bad world, with so much killing? Let us depart."

At that moment my mind pictured me in the bed I lay in rising up into a cylindrical black tube, leading in the air to daylight at the end of it. I left the bed and was being gently vacuumed up the black cylinder unit, and rising up and reaching a third of the way I began to protest, (to whom?) saying, "This is not fair! (I could still hear the noise of the artillery cannons.) This is not fair! I am only twenty years old. I have not started to live yet. I have not seen my sister's new baby. This is going to hurt my mother! THIS IS NOT FAIR!"

Then I commenced descending slowly floating down the black cylinder.

I awakened and adopted my excruciating pains of my wounds. Morphine or medication to kill the pain for a few hours helped but the pain did not subside for some months without pain killers.

A few days later I was transported by ambulance to a seaside airfield we had captured and I was loaded onto a DC3 Aircraft with double tear bunks along each side of the plane. Each bunk was loaded with wounded with some sitting on the floor. The plane had to strain to get airborne with the wounded on the bunks strapped down because of the heavy swaying of the aircraft.

The loading door of the DC3 could not be closed so we flew with it open. I could hear the load engines and smell of fish over the water of the English Channel.

We were transported to a Canadian military hospital in England that was packed with wounded, many from my Regiment.

As soon as we arrived, they placed a heater over my raw stomach to dry it up and form skin. This contraction had its light turned off at nights for sleeping. The heater however picked up extra heat. I didn't complain, I screamed, "Get this thing off of me!"

A week of so later, I along with others were transferred to another military hospital called Watford, located near London. This was where all the documentation arrangements were prepared to sail you home to Canada. The transfer raised the moral a little.

I had visits to my bedside by many of my buddies from the Royals who were able to motivate around on their own or wheelchairs. My lifelong friend and buddy Peter Walsh had two cousins, the Rogers sisters, residing in the city of London, who came to visit us twice. They escorted us around the hospital area. Attending the local entertainment in a wheelchair was a great moral boaster. I shall always remember their kindness to me.

At all times, especially while squared by lady friends, I suffered a constant threat and fear that my colostomy attached to my stomach was ready to excrete excrement at any moment without notice, causing me great embarrassment.

My friend and buddy Peter Walsh, left for home to Canada before me. However, I thanked God for small mercies. I felt a trickle of life coming back into me, and hearing that I was scheduled for the next hospital ship for home helped some.

A month or so later, much to my delight, I was being prepared for transport to a hospital ship bound for Canadian soil. However, I was disappointed when the soft, warm Salvation Army housecoat, that had rendered me much physical comfort and aided in my recovery, was removed off my back. I had thought it was a gift to keep. I was so sick, weak and helpless, not unlike a child having his soother taken out of his mouth.

Chapter 36

SAILING BACK TO CANADA

I was stretchered onto a military ambulance for an extensive drive to the seashore, and then onto white coloured ship with a large red cross of each side of the ship and high on the smoke stack.

Shortly thereafter, we could hear the pull of the heavy chains setting the ship free to drift off the shore of Great Britain.

It was winter 1944-45. The struggle with the war continued. But for me and most of us onboard the ship the war was over. I have become redundant for military service and I could not foresee how I would become useful to myself.

To gain strength, a long rest period was mandatory. Thereafter I faced several surgical operations to mend and recuperate physically my shattered body. Then followed the excessive physiotherapy required to learn to walk all over again and adjust to a plastic splint support for my right foot which aided me, and still aids me to walk. I was left permanently paralyzed from the knee down on the right leg. My left foot had shrapnel removed but besides the scar it held up okay. In my stomach I am missing two feet of bowel damaged by shrapnel. The right side of my rib cage is wired together, to support the lung and intestines. The larger pieces of shrapnel in my scull were surgically removed but there are the tiny pieces still embedded in my scull which were too deep in to remove. But so far, have given me no trouble. On my left hand the forefinger and thumb were not injured but the three fingers that stopped flying shrapnel are paralyzed. However I do have the full use of my arm. On my lower back, I stopped a hot, spent piece of shrapnel that seared the lower vertebrae but has not given me problems, only a scar, five inches in diameter, on the lower part of the spine.

The ship was saturated with wounded military personnel representing the three services but with emphasis on the Army Infantry.

Men were moaning in bed with pain covered in bandages in various forms, some with casts on their arms and legs and others like myself were not permitted to move too for fear of too much bleeding.

One chap across from my bed commented that we are finished. He said, "My father was a doctor in the first war. He said the wounded don't last long. They don't live past the age of fifty years."

The soldier had had a leg blown off and was very depressed and very mad about his predicament.

He was wearing the Royal Regiment insignia patch on his tunic. I asked what Company was he with. He said he was with "C" company. I remarked that I was in Charley, (C Company). "I don't remember you."

He replied, "I was not there long. One day. I was attached to the Royals in the morning and was stretchered out late that afternoon with my leg missing."

Speaking from experience there is no exercise that trains you to meet the front line horror of an Infantry soldier. The emersion into the battle field is twenty-four hours a day, week in week out with no relief. It is excruciating. Waiting to be instantly killed, or wounded at any moment or become a prisoner of war. There is no other choice available to you in the battlefield. When it is your turn to receive one or more pieces of white-hot shrapnel it is excruciatingly painful and, at that moment, the very first thought that flows though your mind is, "I am free of the frontline battle. And I don't have to go back in."

Perhaps that thought gave me the strength to survive my many wounds.

You kill or be killed. Slaughtering boys eighteen and nineteen years of age such as yourself. You have no other choice. But it is exposing the animal in the young man forced to commit inhumanity to man. To compound the cruelty of war, when advancing towards the enemy, it is an "order" you do not stop to aide your wounded buddy. You die alone.

There are two categories in the military service; those who fire the guns and those soldiers who pass the ammunition. Both are important elements. But let's recognize the difference and render credit accordingly.

Now I go back to my tale.

The hospital ship was a converted ocean liner, that had travelled the Atlantic Ocean, between England, France and North America in peace time. It was called "The Empress of Britain" and most of its decks were changed into open wards.

You may recall that not too long ago, my father had up-rooted me from my comfortable settled ways of a kid's lifestyle from Macedonia to make a better life for his family in Canada, and that this was the ship that brought me to Canada!

At the time though, the above thought had very little impact on me. I was too sick and was quite content to be on my way home to Toronto, Canada.

It was a six day crossing that grey Atlantic Ocean, with rain and high waves and many prayers by all aboard for a safe crossing. Each two-hour period, one could hear the ship's foghorn, and the Morse Code signalling the enemy crafts, as to who we are, where we were bound and how many wounded and crew onboard ship. We also let them know we were carrying no fire-arms nor ammunition. We are available for boarding and inspection.

We finally reached the Port of Halifax. It was the same port, with the train tracks parallel to the ship's dock, making it easy for embarking and disembarking. It was mid-winter and cold, with heavy snow covering the ground. But it did not take long to be stretchered onto the rail cars that were equipped with bunk beds (upper and lower) and ample heat circulating for comfort in the rail car.

As the train rolled westward, ice formed around the frame and fogged up the windows, making it difficult to see that frozen bare trees and the beautiful soil of Canada.

We disembarked some stretcher cases in New Brunswick and then made two more stops in the province of Quebec. Finally we made a bee line to Toronto, rolling directly into a covered area of the Canadian National Exhibition grounds.

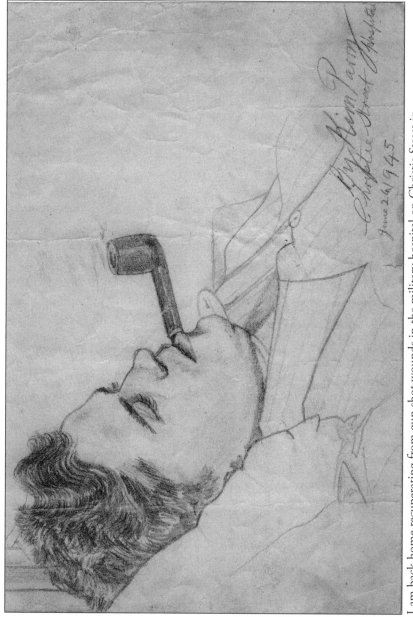

I am back home recuperating from gun shot wounds in the military hospital on Christie Street in Toronto, June 26, 1945.

Chapter 37

HOME

The city of Toronto's mayor was in attendance and welcomed us home, speaking to the bed-ridden patients through a loud speaker.

We were then stretchered onto ambulance, directly to Chorley Park Hospital over-looking the Bloor Street bridge. The hospital was a converted residence of the son of Governor George Grave Simcoe. There I was first met and greeted by my family.

My poor loving mother viewed my one leg in a cast. I was sitting on the bed, with my thin good leg tucked under me almost out of sight. My mother drew the conclusion it was lost in the war! The poor dear tried to encourage me, "Oh well, you have one good leg," pointing to the leg with the cast on it.

Trying to avoid the shock on her face, I quickly pulled my good leg from under me to show her I had my two legs. And I told her that the cast would be off in a little while. She cried she was so happy to see me survive the ordeal.

My dear mother died three years later, at the age of fifty-two years. I know I must have been a contributory factor in shortening her life. She passed away in my father's automobile. I was driving and my mother was sitting in between my father and me, with my aunt and two cousins, Philip and Jim occupying the rear seat. We were out for a Sunday drive when we stopped at our destination, Lake Wilcox. Mother looked worried or in pain but she did not reveal to anyone in that present company. Overlooking the little lake, sitting on a picnic table beside my dear mother Nenka, she had a brief, private conversation with me, asking me, "You are okay now?"

I replied, "Don't worry so much, Ma. I am okay now."

Later, returning home from Lake Wilcox, she quietly stopped breathing while she was sitting beside me and my crying father.

I do hope God saw fit to bless my good mother Nenka.

We drove my mother's body directly to the funeral parlour, located couple of blocks north of my father's restaurant. I went into the funeral parlour, leaving my father and my aunt and her two crying children in the car, and phoned our doctor. The funeral director came out to the car and placed my mother's limp body on a stretcher and rolled it into the funeral home.

The next day I was stricken with so much grief, I found myself at Union Station, purchasing a ticket on the next train leaving the station. I found myself in Cobourg, Ontario. I do not recollect where I spent the night. Then panic-stricken, I thought, "I must get back for my mother's funeral!"

I didn't have any money left, so I hitch-hiked back home. It took most of the day.

On the highway with my thumb out, I witnessed a tractor trailer that had lost one of its wheels, come furiously rolling down the highway passing the truck driver and forcing him to slam on his brakes to stop and retrieve the loosened huge tire.

After two or three car hikes, I landed in Toronto. The last driver let me off right in front of the restaurant.

The funeral was the next day. I attended the vigil at the funeral home that evening. The whole family and all our relatives attending the interment were heartbroken, especially my father, who seldom expressed stress or any emotion towards my mother.

He asked the funeral driver of the hearse to drive by our restaurant and our apartment which was located above it. With a tear in his eyes he mumbled something like "This is your last time, Nenka."

Thereafter, our little humble home above the store was never the same, just us three bachelors, my father, my brother and me.

I had just completed about fourteen months of uncomfortable medical treatment in the military hospital on Christie Street in Toronto and was released facing a blank future, not knowing what and where to proceed.

I was set up with a leg support, for my paralyzed drop foot. It fit into my shoe, to prevent me from tripping over my paralyzed dropped foot. I wear a version of this apparatus to this day.

I attempted to return to school established especially for veterans to complete their studies and to help them proceed with some kind of career. Many of us failed in this endeavour, I being one of them. It was a condensed course; a six month attempt to complete a two-year academic course for a diploma. It was a desperate attempt on my part and when I failed miserably because of a mental block I was called in by the Department of Veterans Affairs. I was asked the reason why and I could not give them an answer.

Maybe I was too old for school. Besides I never did shine in academic work. But I sincerely tried hard in those six months. My mind was not open to learning!

I condemned myself quite severely, which did not help the situation. Saying to myself, I was just plain stupid. I had no answer.

The Department of Veterans Affairs suggested and referred me to a psychiatrist.

I was diagnosed as suffering with Shell Shock. Post Traumatic Stress Syndrome is the modern medical term for it today.

They recommended that I should put off schooling until my head cleared. I asked when that would be. The doctor said he did not know and that it could take anywhere from ten months to ten years to get over shell shock.

Even though the doctor's diagnosis revealed the problem, nevertheless I was still very depressed. I so wished I could please my father and his chiding me about returning to school did not help me much. I hesitated to tell father about the psychiatrist. When I did, he said, "We'll have to train you as a dishwasher!" (His comment sounds worse in the Macedonian language.)

I was living under my father's roof and unable to support myself. I was always cognizant of my father maintaining me for most of my twenty-two years. It bothered me somehow. I knew he could not afford it and it made an impact on me. It indicated nil personal progress and helped me to consider myself a loser. I was helpless.

Chapter 38

RUNNING AWAY

I had to leave.

I saw an ad in the help-wanted column in the newspaper offering a free trip to the west coast in exchange for help with driving. I was capable of that function. The following week, I was on my way westward, destination Vancouver, with three people including the driver. We didn't do any driving. The man had just wanted company on the three day motor drive to Vancouver. Or after meeting us he didn't trust us behind the wheel!

The chap that arranged delivery of the auto to Vancouver for free was Toronto-born of Ukrainian decent. It was employment for him. He was returning by bus back to Toronto to pick up another auto for delivery.

On the way, we stopped to say hello to a relative of his who lived in the backwoods of British Columbia. His house was dilapidated shack. We sat outside, with the trees overlapping his house. The visit took less then an hour and we were soon on our way, with the host saying come back and visit again.

The other fellow who thought he could help with the driving was approximately thirty years of age. He was going west looking for a job in automobile motor repairs. Just fresh in from England, this concerned dedicated fellow was eager to find employment and send for his family.

The third passenger was, of course, me and I didn't know why I was going or what I was going to do when we reached our destination. Talk about a lost soul. This was my first visit west.

We arrived in Vancouver and we delivered the used automobile to a garage, as the driver was instructed to do. The three of us parted company there. The driver was on his way to the bus depot, the English chap went into the same garage to apply for a job in his trade. I saw him as successful. I so wished I was some sort of a mechanic. I would have also asked for work.

We said goodbye. He was visiting relatives and commented that he hoped he could stay with them until he got settled.

I was left alone to look for a place to sleep for the night. The For

Rent column in the Vancouver Sun pointed me to enquire at a rooming house and, once settled in the clean house for the day, I was left to wonder what I was going to do in the city of Vancouver. I was a stranger and knew no one. Talk about being lost.

My sister had her first baby in Vancouver while her soldier husband was stationed in Vancouver. She had the baby christened by a family they lived with and befriended. They were in the restaurant business, so, remembering the name of the business, I soon entered a fairly prosperous looking busy restaurant. Without introducing myself, I ordered lunch then paid the check. (I didn't want them to think I was after a free lunch.) Then I introduced myself and showed them a small photo of their Godchild. We exchanged the usual niceties and since it was noon, the peak lunch hour trade for an eatery, I made haste and left them to look after their business.

I wandered aimlessly around the city of Vancouver, thinking about my conversation with those good people who were proprietors of a prosperous restaurant.

Why didn't I seek advice and direction for employment in that city instead of shutting myself out by saying I was just passing through and I was on my way home to Toronto?

That same day I found myself at the bus depot and by night I sat depressed, as the bus went rumbling down the main highway for the long trip back to Toronto.

Chapter 39

THE RESTAURANT BUSINESS

Some months later my good cousin Alex Trenton approached me regarding going into partnership in the restaurant business. He had found a building with a restaurant on the bottom floor on Queen Street, east of Yonge Street.

Cousin Alex was also a veteran who saw action in Italy and Holland in the Tank Corp. After being blown out of his tank he married the lovely Grace. Although she was a war bride from Scotland she had taught herself to cook and speak like a Macedonian. They raised three boys and two girls. They were a lovely family.

We proceeded investigating that building that was housing the restaurant. For a portion of the down payment we were to receive from Veteran Affairs, as rehabilitation settlement for all service personnel, the rest was to be a bank loan. The balance was held as a large mortgage with the hopes the business would generate enough revenue to pay all debts accrued plus render some living expenses.

It was a very serious, sober time trying to figure out how we were to assemble the funds to turn this into a reality. None of us were flushed with funds.

It was not a pleasant adventure. We were unable to arrange financing and I was sorry. It was a good opportunity for us to make a start but the owner of the property had accepted another offer pending. Hearing this however, along came my brother-in-law seeking a partnership with me. (My sister's husband, Louis, was the one who was stationed in Vancouver, where his first child was born.) Neither my cousin nor my brother-in-law, were aware of my Post Traumatic Stress Syndrome and of course I didn't mention it to them but neither did I attempt to keep it a secret. I now felt no pain from it so I had put it out of my memory.

We did much dreaming and shopping for a good restaurant location. Most of what we wished for we could not afford.

Several months had passed since my cousin's war bride, the lovely Grace, had arrived from Scotland and Alex decided he'd put his veterans establishment money into purchasing a home.

My brother-in-law and I kept looking and one day he phoned to say there was a location he wanted me to investigate. It was a very busy lunch counter on Yonge Street. We very much wished to purchase it but upon further investigating we discovered that the restaurant owner was selling because he had only three years remaining on the lease. This was unsuitable since it would require that much time to pay our debts and more. We required and therefore applied to the landlord for a ten-year lease, unsuccessfully, so we reluctantly abandoned that idea.

Our problem was not finding a location; it was locating one within our financial power to borrow the funds from the bank. Our collateral was very limited.

A month or so later, my brother-in-law phoned, with enthusiasm in his voice, about a location in the middle of the University of Toronto that was for sale. The two gay, male owners of the restaurant had purchased it less then a year previously. So, why were they selling? The reason, they gave us was irreconcilable differences, plus it was too far to travel from their residence Oakville to work. We decided to purchase the business but complications set in. We did not have enough funds to close the deal. The bank had limits for people with our financial stability and would not budge for any additional funds. So we had to take on a silent partner, Mike, a cousin of my brother-in-law, who had rendered advice, and encouraged us to purchase this restaurant. He, Mike Mergalis, invested 33% of the funds required making us all equal partners.

We discovered after buying the business that the previous owners thought the University of Toronto closed down for the summer. We, being green, became very concerned that we have been "taken in". Even opening that first morning for business as proprietors we didn't know how green we were. We were not seeking to make a fortune! Just to try and eke out a living. Finding a location, we could financially afford, required considerable effort so we overlooked many details. We were fortunate to purchase the restaurant with the raw food supplies on the premises and cigarette stock left from the previous owners to keep us going until we were able to contact and establish ourselves with the suppliers as the new owners.

Entering the world of business was an exciting and stressful period in my life!

Oops! Another oversight! No cash for change in the register. It was 6:30 a.m. and banks opened at 10:00 a.m. Just becoming aware of this important detail, we emptied our pockets of coins and bills. Just at that moment, Gus, the husband of my favourite cousin Helen, walked into the restaurant with his delivery of loads of fresh bread. The dear man not only provided us with bread but when he heard of our dilemma he walked over to the till (cash register) and deposited rolls of coins and bills amounting to fifty dollars. He said, "I don't want it back. This is to wish you luck!"

We then discovered that summer school was open, plus the local trade kept us alive. Come September, our noon hour trade came to life and kept us going and meeting our expenses and obligations.

We opened for breakfast at 6:00 a.m. Lunch was from11:30 a.m. to 2:00 p.m. and supper was 5:00 p.m. to 7:30 p.m. The evening trade ran until midnight. Louis and I split up the day and alternated shifts bi-monthly. Our staff consisted of a chef and a Night Cook, and one dish-washer. The night cook cleaned up and did the dishes. We had two wait-resses for days and two waitresses for nights. If any employee did not show for work, my partner and I filled in. (Which was quite often.)

We had many students from around the world that frequented our restaurant so we purchased a huge hard cover register with lined pages. Titled under the word "REGISTER WE SERVE THE WORLD". Above each blank page was DATE:_____. NAME:_____.COUN-TRY:_____. GRADUATING DATE:_____.

It was amazing how many foreign students came in to sign the register.

While the restaurant was up and running we turned our attention to a second business venture. It came in the form of promoting our coleslaw and potato salad.

One day a student praised our potato salad. He was dining at the time with his father who suggested we package it and sell to the grocery stores. So we did just that. I had business cards printed that read: SCS (Students Coffee Shop) "We serve the world" 25 Harbord St. I bought four containers with lids that our chef, Mr. Bill Ohashi, filled and decorated. We had two containers of cold slaw with a sliver of red radish on top in the center of clear lid and two containers of potato salad with a dash of paprika and a sprig of green parsley on top. Then I stamped the top of the lids with a red rubber stamp we used on the bank deposit slips.

Proceeding blindly with much trepidation in my dilapidated car I went to sell my wares to the great Dominion and A&P Grocery Stores.

After completing my interview with them, I deposited my trial samples of coleslaw and potato salad with them.

They finished the brief encounter with, "We will let you know."

At this juncture, our silent partner, Mike Mergalis, being of the old school, was becoming a bit concerned that we were wondering off into a strange field and neglecting the restaurant. This was not true. We needed the revenue from the restaurant to keep us afloat in our new venture, which we thought had good potential.

At the conclusion of our talk, he wanted out so we borrowed the funds from the bank and paid him off with a $700 profit. It was a good investment for him and we parted friends.

A week passed as we waited in anticipation to hear from the only two major grocery chains on the city. There was no response. Oh well, we didn't invest much in the venture. We could not afford more since we were just scraping to meeting the loan payments. Who did we think we were anyway?

Further information on our potato/coleslaw venture came via the phone requesting our food costs on both the potato salad and coleslaw and other pertinent questions. Who were we? How long had we been in business? And other such questions. We submitted all the answers to the best of our ability, along with a covering letter, and mailed it registered mail. And waited and waited.

On a Friday we received a phone call. (I was on the night shift.) My brother-in-law received the message to call me at home. We had to start delivery on Monday, pick up a list of the stores locations, before we closed that day. I was so overwhelmed. We were so busy patting ourselves on the back that we forgot we had no supplies to go into production on Monday so we made arrangements for the delivery required to commence and the staff to produce the product.

The A&P Stores did not contact us. Oh well, we had our hands full anyway.

Come mid-week though, The A&P Stores phoned to ask us to start deliveries next week to all the stores in the city, on Tuesdays and Thursday only.

There was so much to quickly be assembled. We rented a panel truck, hired a driver to deliver. Then we needed to construct and organize a separate production kitchen to prepare and assemble the salads. Once that was done, we had to call the city health inspector to pass it for production. It was painted high white gloss, for easy maintenance, with a see-through window covering the front of the kitchen. I converted most of the restaurant basement into preparation kitchen, and supply area for the bulk potatoes and cabbage supply.

We were lucky to have an entrance to the back of the restaurant with a direct entrance to the basement to receive supplies and loading the panel truck for delivery, without interrupting the restaurant operation.

In the meantime, all preparation was carried out in the restaurant kitchen at nights.

First thing we ordered was a walk-in refrigerator to store the prepared salads ready for transport and to alleviate the chaos of the restaurant refrigerators. I made a quick run to Detroit, Michigan, and purchased a manual potato cutter that sliced a boiled potato into cubes. It was a dandy labour-saving device, and helped with the consistency and improved the appearance of the product.

As if there wasn't enough to keep me busy at this time I was also involved with evening school classes. As I mentioned previously, my attempt at obtaining a high school diploma was, much to my regret, still a failure. Therefore, I resorted to night school and attended classes when it was not interfering or causing me to neglect my business. Some of the courses I took at Ryerson Technical School included Business Accounting (which has held me in good stead to this day) and Commercial Cooking. I never indulged nor had the desire to cook but needed the knowledge to employ competent chefs.

At this stage of my business career since I didn't had much spare time for school I only took courses that I felt were necessary and could provide me with knowledge that I would derive benefit at that period of time.

My partner was not interested in enhancing his knowledge of the catering business. He was dismayed with it since he was a family man and the financial advancement was slow. He complained and was sorry he terminated his employment with the CN Railway to enter into the restaurant business. It was his wife, my sister, who coerced him into it. She didn't want him coming home with dirty hands. (Although she didn't mind receiving the fat paycheque that came with it.) Above all she didn't want him to be classed as a labourer.

With this busy time in my life, even though I had lady friends and acquaintances and the odd social evening, I could not afford to think seriously of marriage, kids, a home and all that went with it. I was also learning that in this business you learn to smile to your patrons and not expose your burdens. The restaurant business is a difficult one and very hard to derive a profit from. The hours are long and the public is frustrating to deal with. The owner of the restaurant suffers from constant pilfering and food deterioration. It is not like the retail hardware business. If you steal a hammer or a screwdriver you're satisfied. Not so in the food catering game. If the worker takes a pound of butter or a few slices of meat home he will need some more or another food item tomorrow.

Just make sure the Boss is not looking. The employee feels justified in taking it. This has saved him money. He feels he deserves it since the boss "don't pay me enough wages".

As a lesson learned, in retrospect, if one can borrow the capital, I would advise him to purchase the property housing the restaurant. You will suffer equally operating the restaurant with or without owning the property. If the building is not available to you, don't buy the business.

Back to my tale…

The second season in the potato/coleslaw business venture, we were fortunate to bid on and were successfully granted the ability to supply both of the major stores. I was elated. This meant we could amend some of the commitment that cost us dearly. These terms included:

1. No returns. Stores should only order what they could sell for the week.

2. No deliveries directly to the stores refrigerator. (Salads never reached the front of the store unless a customer asked for it.) I requested space in the store and our driver delivered and displayed the product.

Now we were ready to concentrate on canvassing for new business. This would enable us to pay off the equipment and the conversion of the basement into a food processing plant. The second season terminated quite successfully with the usual trials and tribulations but with some additional headway. We were looking forward to supplying them next year.

The third year we lost our tender to our competitor, the famous corned beef house restaurant of Toronto. No sooner we were advised by telephone of our unsuccessful bid then who should walk into my establishment? Mr. Sam Shopsowitz, the Corned Beef King.

I sat beside him at the counter. Quietly I asked, "What do you want? Congratulations, or did you come in to gloat?"

He replied, "No. I have a proposition for you. I would like you to make the potato salad and coleslaw and pack it under my banner. I'll supply you with my containers and lids. At present, the construction of my factory is not finished and I have nowhere to process or pack this stuff. My truck will come, pick up and deliver. What do you say?"

After some discussion on the matter, we came to a desirable agreement. I must say it was the most profitable season we ever had.

Come the following season we submitted a tender, went through the same procedure but were unsuccessful. Mr. Sam Shopsowitz's processing plant was in full working order. He was well ensconced with the two major grocery chains. Today, he has more than a dozen food products that he has been selling to grocery stores for many years. Sam supplied the purchasers and head office personnel with lots of perks. He entertained and gave sports tickets and gifts to the ones that counted to add favouritism to his submission. For these and other reasons I am not aware of, they always favoured his products.

This was the year my father's brother and partner, after many years working together, dissolved their partnership in their restaurant and divided the two little side by side retail buildings, they purchased together. I think this was due to my father advanced age and drinking, on-and-off the job. They decided who would take which building by the flip of a coin. My father was left with the building housing the restaurant.

My uncle, with a younger (fresh in from the old country) nephew, formed a partnership and purchased a small garage-sized building on York Street in downtown Toronto. It was a good busy location with shorter hours and always closed on Sundays.

My father was left alone to operate his restaurant. As he continued drinking the business deteriorated. The sanitation was neglected, due to his eye problems and finally a customer informed the health department of the city. The restaurant was closed down until he brought up the standard of sanitation. The long hours of labour over many years and his eyes sight deteriorating, required an eye operation. The health inspector contacted me and apprised me of my father's situation. My sister checked my father in hospital for his eye surgery and I left my business with my partner to carry on, while I commenced a clean-up operation of my father's restaurant.

Front of Trenton Grill, dining room staff, me, uncle Basil and sister Christine, 1941.

I managed the Trenton Grill for one and a half years because of my father's poor health, 1953.

21 Harbord St. Main entrance of Students' Coffee Shop, 1949.

The interior of the Students' Coffee Shop with the basement floor premises being utilized for manufacturing potato salad and coleslaw for Dominion and A & P grocery stores.

Chapter 40

MY THIRD BUSINESS VENTURE

My father's restaurant required considerable cleaning and kitchen renovations. I poured my total personal savings to bring the restaurant up to inspection standard and permit me to re-open the business. Following the eye surgery my father stayed with my sister for a few days. He was keen on returning to his home above the restaurant, and to witness the re-opening. He wanted to see his life's work rejuvenated and check in on the first day's revenue. He was so pleased he even congratulated me. This was the very first time he ever said a favourable word to me on any matter!

It became obvious to me that with my fathers' heavy alcohol consumption continuing, he was no longer fit to operate his restaurant. Therefore I came to the conclusion that I should sell my father's business to create a rental income for him. He could live above the store and I would return to my own business. He agreed with my suggestion. However, it required much more time than I had estimated to sell Dad's restaurant. Even with advertising and all, it took a total of two years. In the meantime I was thirty-one years old and it was time (not that I was prepared) that the appropriate person came along and I married her. Pearl Patskou was just the kind of feisty, energetic girl I thought I needed in my very busy life. She helped sporadically in the restaurant until she discovered I couldn't afford to pay her a salary. She quickly got a job at the bank across the street. Also I could not rely on my father's help, due to his alcoholism, so I hired a cook I could not afford. That period of time was not a bowl of cherries for me.

My partner was not happy with me for deserting him, (I had been gone now for over two years) and could not wait for my return. He disliked the restaurant game, and was anxious to get out of it. I was left with no choice but to tell him to put our restaurant for sale. It was my misfortune, that my Students Coffee Shop sold first. I would have liked (as I had planned) to have bought my partner's share and kept my restaurant. It was a better location with more potential, and I still had hope in building up the salad sideline. But I was trapped. I had invested all my personal savings into rejuvenating my father's business. And even if I could borrow the funds to buy my partner out I could not leave my father in his condition until I sold his business. Only then he would have some security and income by renting the restaurant and living above it.

Two years went by. I continued the advertising to sell the restaurant, and finally, I accepted the first offer for the Trenton Grill Restaurant. The money changed hands leaving me with no business of any kind and no funds.

Chapter 41

JOB HUNTING

I thought I had had enough of the food business and I would try a different line of work. Actually I had no choice. I could not return to working in the catering business. That would confirm in my view and others that I have become a loser. No, I had too much pride to admit it to myself. This is the reason I did not pursue the catering game and turfed myself out of self-employment game, like I did in high school at sixteen years of age.

I needed a job immediately. My wife had terminated her employment with the bank some months ago, so we had no money coming in. Scanning the employment ads, I applied for work with the Grannell Company who manufactured safety hardware and flanges. My job was to receive orders over the phone from customers, then quote a price and delivery time. It was in a large area full of desks performing the same tasks.

My wife said, "You are not going to be happy at that work!"

She was right, three months later I was fired.

I then applied for employment with the Blind Institute as a Supervisor training the partially blind people to make and give change to customers, etc. I was fairly satisfied with the position until I got my head cleared and realized exactly how much future there was with that job.

Then came a problem with a large food contract they had with a lumber mill and processing plant in Kapuskasing, Ontario. They asked me to go up and take management of three cafeterias outside this large town. Needing the job, I agreed to go up and operate the units until I found and trained a manager, but I would not stay permanently. I did not want to be stationed up there. They declined my suggestion, and I was out of a job. I probably would have accepted the north location, but my wife was adamant she was not going up into the wilds of the north Ontario.

The third job I found was with Nation Wide Food Services. Back in the catering field. I applied to an American company, who had recently established an office in Toronto. Mr. Charles Martin was the Vice President, who successfully tendered to feed cadets in summer camps for the provinces of Ontario and Saskatchewan. I was hired to take over the operation in Saskatchewan at Camp Dundurn located on the outskirts of Saskatoon, for the period of May to September. Then I was to have a choice to either go to work in the United States, out of Chicago head-quarters or return to Toronto head office.

Before leaving for Dundurn, Saskatchewan, it was suggested by the Vice President that I join them to help entertain some high ranking Officers coming in from Ottawa and to interview the two Managers plus meet the VP.

The Americans really had the business savvy. There in his elabo-rately furnished apartment, in the posh Yonge and St Clair area, the pas-tries, delicate sandwiches and beverages had just arrived, with a waitress ready to serve. Charley said to me, he just moved in that morning.

The two Brigadiers arrived shortly thereafter. There were only three of us. Charley, the manager for Camp Chipawa, Ontario, and myself. After the introductions coffee and tea was poured, and the wait-ress continually passed the sandwiches and pastries on a silver tray, while Charley the V.P. continued with his spiel on how much he loved Canada, how his family was on their way up here, last week he had reg-istered his son for Upper Canada College, etc. etc. And how he was most eager to become a Canadian citizen.

The Canadian Officers left shortly after lunch. Mr. Charley Martin assured them the season would be successfully carried out to the letter of the contract agreement. I never saw those two officers again. They were stationed in Ottawa. Not one person inspected nor toured the mess halls, except the orderly officer posted in the camp.

Charley Martin gave the officers the impression the apartment was his permanent residence. In fact, he moved out that afternoon. It was a one day rental agreement. Also the office he rented included the furni-ture and the secretaries' reception area. He occupied it until the termina-tion of the Cadet contract. If he could have attracted more business he would had prolonged the lease, but he was not that fortunate, so when I returned to Toronto he had pulled up stakes and returned to Chicago.

On our way out west, I was driving the same old Chevy. I won-dered if it would get us to our destination. I thought we might have been better off if we accepted transfer to operate the food service in Kapuskasing with the Blind Institute, since we were heading much further from our home. And with Dad in Toronto, I was not sure how he was fairing out with his tenant operating the restaurant.

I did not mention any of this to Pearl. She was upset enough at having to leave her mother and sisters behind. It was her first trip so far away from home and it made her very uneasy and she was a highly strung person by nature.

The route travelling west took us north around Lake Superior. What beautiful country and scenery is in that area of northern Ontario and crossing into the province of Manitoba. It was our first time west together. On the second day we arrived in Camp Dundurn, Saskatchewan. It was late in the evening and my wife was moaning and complaining that she missed Toronto. As the darkness fell abruptly, we were lost in the camp. Leaving Pearl in the car, I went into a noisy Officer's pub to enquire about the Camp Commandant, whom I had learned had gone to Saskatoon for the evening. Minutes later I returned to the car. Pearl was hyperventilating with fear. She wanted us to return to Toronto; head home that night. Instead I headed for the town of Dundurn, a short distance away, to the only hotel and rented a room. Pearl still was moaning for home as we got settled in the room. I became somewhat irritated with my wife complaints. I agreed to take my wife to the station either that night or first thing in the morning, but I had to stay to honour out my contract with the Nation Wide Food Services. She did not get along with my father and it was mutual, so I suggested she stay with her Mother until I returned in September. Come morning she was still uncomfortable in the new environment and so was I. Pearl's dissatisfaction with it all prevailed, not making it easier to perform my responsibilities.

There was a mess hall in operation by the Army which was assigned over to me and taken over as soon as my kitchen crew arrived from Toronto. All Chinese lads, from Toronto's Chinatown, good workers, all of them.

The Executive Chef, Phil Swadron, and the Chef, who had the appearance of an alcoholic, were both new to their jobs. The Chef was at constant loggerheads with the Executive Chef. Also arriving was my Assistant Manager, Marty Martin who thought he was manager until finally we phoned Toronto and straightened it out with a long telephone discussion. I made it clear to Charley Martin in Toronto that co- management would not work. "You choose, Charley" I said. "If he is the manager, I am on my way back."

I assigned the Assistant Manager in charge of the Officers Mess and the Sergeants Mess. He soon ran into difficulty with the Camp Commandant. The Assistant Manager's German attitude and accent did not help him very much. He was on his way back to Toronto. The staff I hired locally was an unsettled diverse group of human beings. Except for the Chinese staff, the rest of the staff was forced to work together for fear of being cut off their pay cheque. I did just that with two employees to weed out the most troublesome.

The Executive Chef caused more havoc then the rest of them. He was under the impression he was running a food service in a luxury hotel with ample and available help. The chefs in the three kitchens refused to work with him. All orders had to come from him through me, making my burden much heavier. I brought him up on the carpet more times then any other employee. On a couple of occasions we came close to physical blows. He also boasted of his authority in the Officers Mess one night. The Officer could not find me. He phoned directly to my head office in Toronto and he was on his way and out of a job.

I was now left with no Assistant Manager and no Executive Chef. And I had to feed 1,800 Cadets plus staff three times daily. No easy task to say the least. I had no host in the Officers Dining Room, so I paid a visit when I could. I soon placed my wife on the payroll as hostess in the Dining Room both to occupy her and to build up our very low saving account.

I employed a local student in the office to do the payroll of the forty-eight employees and I did the daily rounds in each kitchen and the feeding of the cadets in overnight bivouac training. Come the first of September, our contract with the Department Of Defence was honoured and the cadets had returned home. It was not an easy five months and it was a great relief when it was over.

The Army, as agreed, was kind enough to supply transportation for my employees to the railway station in Saskatoon. I saw them off and bid the farewell with a "see you in Toronto."

We said our goodbyes to the Camp Commandant and his wife. We were neighbours as his tent was next to ours. Also we said goodbye to the Regimental Sergeant Major, who was very kind and understanding to my wife, in the Officer's Dining Room.

Then, to comply with the contract with a member of the military, we checked and returned all kitchen and equipment belonging to the Army,

I was up early in the morning with Pearl, packed and ready to travel home. Overlooking an empty campsite, only a small, permanent, military staff was present, with not many in the mess hall. We had breakfast. I can still see in my mind eye, a permanent fat unshaven soldier cook, over a large grill turning sausages and a deep pot of soggy scrabbled eggs on the side. Both he and his breakfast looked so unappetizing.

My staff at the Military Cadet Camp located in Dundurn, Saskatchewan. I am located in the middle with my wife Percy to my left.

Chapter 42

RETURNING HOME

Hearing nothing from the head office in Toronto about a permanent job as I was promised I commented to my wife there is nothing for us back home, except her arguing with my Dad. I suggested we head west to Vancouver with our savings so we could start a fresh. She was adamant about returning home and would not hear of it. She missed her family too much. So, we commenced heading east, for Toronto.

On the road we stopped off for the night. I can't remember if it was before or after Winnipeg. Anyway, after supper we attended carnival in that town. I was mesmerized with a car trinket the barker was peddling to a crowd of people milling in front of him. He was flogging a round screen item that fits over the carburetor of your car and it improved your gas mileage by 25 %. Having a long distance to drive for Toronto I could use the gas savings so the next morning I had the trinket installed. Keeping careful check on the gas consumption for the total day, the results were a large, big, fat zero. Oh well, I didn't spend much on the invention.

We decided to detour into the US. Heading for Chicago, I was curious to see the headquarters of the Nation Wide Food Service Corp. When we located the street, I suggested to Pearl she stay in the car. No was her answer. Pearl wished to come in. We entered this multi-story building, walking to the overused elevator, then onto a floor and into a room where there was a counter dividing the reception area and the office personnel.

We introduced ourselves and a asked for Mr. Martin. A minute later, out came one of the clerks. He said "I am Martin."

We replied, "No, Mr. Charles Martin."

They looked a bit stunned and some other person came out said, "He is not here."

I said, "We are on the way to Toronto. Say hello to him for us."

"Too bad he's not around. He would have taken you out for lunch."

"We've had lunch. Thank you. Goodbye"

Driving out of Chicago we found it odd that they would not be familiar the name of their Vice President.

Oh well. Next stop, Toronto.

On arrival, Persephone [Pearl] was filled with emotions. She asked me to detour through her old district Weston Road and drive east along St Clair to cover the area she grew up in. We passed her father's building which housed his restaurant where she had worked for a while. Since they lived in that area, I had suggested dropping her off at her parent's house, for a visit. She declined.

Reaching our domicile, which was actually my father's home over the restaurant, I was grateful he was out (I assume the beverage room). This gave us an opportunity to settle in. When Dad did arrive he was in a slightly inebriated state as he welcomed us home. He then commenced complaining that we had left the telephone bill unpaid.

While looking for employment was causing me a lot of concern, I received an odd sort of telephone call from the Ontario Provincial Police, Cobourg Detachment. They asked me if I remembered so and so who worked for me at the Students Coffee Shop. The name was familiar to me. The police officer asked me would I recognize him if I saw him. The police sergeant said they could not locate his next of kin. They presumed he was knocked down hitch-hiking and died on the side of the road where they found him. "We seek your cooperation to identify the body so we can bury him".

A police cruiser picked me up and drove me to the town of Cobourg to identify the body.

I asked how they found out that he worked for me. He said the only identification he had on him was an unemployment book that had my business number.

The next day I called the unemployment office and got my problem cleared. As we talked I brought up my unemployment dilemma. They told me to phone Mr. Kennedy at the Union Station restaurants. They were always looking for help. This was the best employment prospect I had in the two or three weeks back in Toronto. I called Mr. Kennedy and was granted an interview. He toured me around the two restaurant locations at Union Station. Amongst other information he asked me what salary range I was looking for. I blurted out "Seventy-five dollars a week".

I was actually so desperate for work if he had offered me half that much I would have taken it. He said I was thinking along the line of starting me at fifty dollars but he go for sixty dollars weekly and see how it works in a couple of months. I swallowed a couple of times and replied, "It will do to start".

I was asked to report to Mr. Graham at the Malton International Airport Flight Kitchen.

It was a twenty-four-hour, seven-day a week operation. I was to be one of seventeen shift supervisors, who were rotating bi-monthly. I would be working with the chief supervisor for a week who would familiarize me with my duties.

The next day I reported to Mr. Breahart, an ex-Chief Steward with the Royal Dutch Airline. This man familiarized me with the total operation, including the book store, two restaurants, one called the Tea Wing in the Airport complex, the Food Unit operation of the Toronto Flying Club and the main food preparation plant called The Flight Kitchen (the money maker) which provided meals and snacks for all departing aircraft.

Through the week he introduced me to all the supervisors, cashiers, chefs, dishwashers, assembly plant employees, as we walked through all the units that were operated by Aero Caterers (which was later called CARA). Come the end of the week, I was prepared and told my wife that the job entailed shift working. I was ready to start on the midnight shift. Just before leaving for home, Mr. Breahart, my boss, said in his Dutch accent, "I think you better work another week with me".

I said, "Okay".

Driving home I was puzzled. The procedure I had been told was only one week with Mr. Brheart and then I go on rotating shift work. I guessed I haven't got the hang of the job. I didn't understand. I had found the work fascinating that week. Could the boss have discovered my short coming?

That evening I picked up a paper on the way home. After supper, I started reading the Want ads in the Toronto Star. My wife's eagle eyes noticed this and asked, "Why are you looking through the want ads? You have a job!"

I said, "It's a long way to travel to the airport and you never can tell what better situation can be had in the city".

Reporting for work and roaming around the airport with Mr. Breahart I noticed the Shift Managers were being more attentive towards me. I thought they felt sorry for me. I felt sure I'd be gone by the end of the week.

Come the end of the second week the man who hired me from the Union Station was in the office with Mr. Graham, the Branch Manager. I thought they are ready with the axe as Mr. Breahart led me into the office.

The first words I heard were, "Congratulations, you made the grade."

With much inner relief, I thanked them. Then they announced that Mr. Brheart had tendered his resignation a couple of months ago and they were looking for someone to replace him.

They apologized for the roundabout way of testing me and said, "If you had not made the grade we would have offered you a shift supervisor's position and you would have not known what we were up to."

A few months later, Mr. Rod Graham was seconded to develop a new process the company was experimenting with in order to go into mass production of the frozen meal business. He left the airport for his new position that I am not sure he was happy about it.

I was left with 138 employees to perform the duties of both Senior Supervisor and Branch Manager. I performed the responsibilities of these two positions for several months. The company had growing pains with the demand for airport food services and in other areas of a new endeavour that they were involved with.

My domestic situation was rapidly deteriorating between my father and wife. It reached a climax when my father called me aside and told me to "Get out and take your wife with you!"

What was I to do? Should I purchase a house as my wife suggested? It seemed to me I would be devoting all my life in to paying it off. Paying apartment rent with no returns was less appealing.

With the small savings we had from our western venture, plus a bank loan, I placed a down payment on duplex at 191 Castlefield Ave.

Renting one apartment and living in the other turned out very well.

I suggested to my father to come live with us since it was a two-bedroom apartment. He could rent his apartment above the store which was desired by the new owner of the restaurant for additional income. He thanked me, said, "No, it would make your life a double hell."

My father seldom visited my home; only on holidays and only if I picked him up and drove him home. We lived not far from him. I frequently went to visit him without the presence of Pearl. Both were content with that arrangement. My Brother Lazo moved in with Dad as soon as he heard we left. My Dad had company, which gave me some peace of mind even if they were at constant logger heads with each other. Father was cantankerous because of his advanced age and discontentment with life.

My father did not baby-sit with my children. He just came to see his grandchildren and with each visit he had a difference of opinion with Pearl and he stomped off.

Another occasion for a visit and dinner was to view a fourplex I had recently purchased at 1135 Avenue Road, which was located around the corner from my duplex on Castlefield where we lived.

I picked up Dad and we drove to the fourplex building. As we parked in front of it, I asked with a little pride, "What do you think?"

Dad would not get out of the car. He remarked it was an old building and it had been there a long time. Then we went to a waiting supper back on Castlefield. That was it.

Pearl was a good cook and she provided balanced and healthy meals for the family. But Dad was little suspicious of her and what kind of meals she was serving him. The feeling was mutual between daughter-in-law and father-in-law.

On other occasions when picking up Dad for dinner at my house, I'd suggest, with pride, that I show him my two other properties. But Dad always made up some excuse. It was too far to travel, not this time, whatever he could think of. He would stay for supper, have a little wine and the wife's sarcastic, judgemental look, if noticed by my Dad, would cause him stand up and ask me to drive him home. He never had any desire to see my latest "mortgaged-to-the-hilt" acquisitions.

It was not easy living between my Dad and wife. There was something about that contact that set both parties off. Even living in separate domiciles the rift between Dad and my wife never mended.

With my new position as Branch Manager at the airport the responsibilities were heavy, compounding my domestic life. At day's end I drove slowly home, often stopping on a quiet street to smoke my cigar for a few minutes just to clear my head and steel myself to what I was about to encounter at home.

When my children came along, I had a firm hold on the management skills of the job. I cut my hours down from eleven to nine hours most days, for I was eager to get home to see the children. I scheduled to take off each afternoon on Saturday and Sunday. This was the most advantageous time to be away from my work place. Most managers of the airlines take that period of time off, leaving problems in abeyance for Mondays.

My experience operating the food services at the airport requires a separate book. The trials and tribulations of solving the problems of so many employees each had their own unique set of circumstances.

Observing human nature while conversing about daily routine brings to mind a person named Frank who was an assistant to the chef in one of the busy restaurants. He had tendered his two-week notice as he had been offered a job at the airport on a Caribbean Island. He'd recently married and was looking forward to the constant summer weather down there. I wished him luck. A few days later the same cook, appeared at my office requesting a quick run down in operating a flight kitchen airport food service, since this was in fact the job he had accepted. He was going to be branch manger of food services position when he had never held the position in his life. To make a long story short, he was back in three months time.

I have to admire Frank. That did not deter him. He then applied and worked for a prominent catering company in Toronto. They tendered successfully for the new Toronto City Hall, and Frank planned and raised the food standard in the New City Hall. The system he laid out was adopted by future caterers bidding on the city hall contract. Frank ended up vice-president of operations in that catering company.

Another cook, of Portuguese descent, asked me to view a dozen photos of his dead wife at the funeral service and at the interment sight. With tears in his eyes he told me how disappointed he was that his boss (me) had been absent.

After announcing the closing of the famous Avro Aircraft plant located next to the airport, the Prime Minister, John Diefenbaker, walked into the restaurant with a daily paper. He sat of the counter stool reading his paper, of course the airport's Mounted Police were on duty and other security people were stationed unobtrusively at the entrance of the restaurant. My buddy, the Mountie, phoned me and apprised me of the situation. I immediately phoned the hostess on duty. I instructed her to lead Mr. Diefenbaker to our private dining room while I quickly changed into a fresh shirt and tie I had on reserve for such occasions. The Mountie informed me that the hostess walked up to the Prime Minister of Canada and said to him "Mr. Trenton said that you can't sit there. Come with me!"

The Prime Minister of Canada obeyed the hostess' order, asking who is this Mr. Trenton?

Some catastrophes were caused by my decision to solve one. Some were tantamount to me being dismissed of my position if my company could find someone to instantly take over without further disruption. The following is just one of those incidents:

One Friday evening before leaving for home, I walked into the main dining room. All seats were occupied and a long waiting line was at the front entrance of the restaurant. Walking into the kitchen, I noticed that all the kitchen personnel were busy. Walking over to the cooking area I saw that one of the large grills (the size of a dining table) was standing idle. I remembered saying to the chef that fish must not be grilled with meat because they will pick up the odours. But nobody was ordering fish so I instructed the chef to clean the idle grill and start cooking the pork chops and steaks on that grill. "You're, as of right now, out of fish," I said. (With one of the refrigerators full of fish.)

I then went in to the dining room and instructed the hostess to tell the waitresses to tell the customer we were out of fish. That should surely get things moving. The kitchen staff soon saturated the large empty grill with pork chops, steaks and greasy hamburgers. The smoke and grease were being pulled up by the strong exhaust fan, located directly above the grills.

I was pleased with my decision and was ready to go home to my children. Until I witnessed the exhaust fan was drawing up smoke, grease and flames in and out over the exhaust canopy and spreading black smoke into the dining area. The grills were shut off immediately but it had no effect on the fire that was spreading over the kitchen area. We placed towels and aprons under the kitchen doors to prevent the black greasy smoke from spreading all over. Our kitchen fire extinguishers had no effect on the greasy flames just spread it all the more. I asked all the diners to evacuate the dining room with apologies.

The fire departments located both at the airport and the Malton Fire Station seemed to me a long time in coming. As that thought occurred to me, I dashed up the stairs to second floor, where the air traffic controllers were busy directing landing and taking off the aircraft. The black smoke had permeated in this huge area. I approached the chief controller, "You got to get out of here! The dining room is on fire!" At the same moment we could hear the fire engines. The chief controller ordered his staff to leave, and they quickly complied with his order. Then I said, "Dick, you have to leave with me."

He replied, "I can't. There are too many planes above to be brought in."

I went back downstairs. Shortly thereafter the fire department extinguished the fire, leaving the kitchen and the dining room with soot on the floors and black walls.

The local Toronto radio station picked up the story of the fire. Someone from head office staff was sitting at home and heard the broadcast, "Malton Airport in flames!" He phoned me, "Can I help?"

I said, "No, everything is under control".

They didn't realize who started the fire and I didn't reveal who. I was pleased that P.J. Phalen, the owner of the Company was away. I saw him off to New York that day.

What to do now! I thought of the painters who just finished painting the flight kitchen so I was on the phone to the owner, begging to get as many of his crew that night for an overnight paint job. Then I held back all the kitchen staff to start cleaning and scrubbing the kitchen and dining room. I said, "You're all on overtime pay."

The next day, we were ready to open for breakfast in the morning at 9:00 a.m. instead of the usual 6:00 a.m. opening.

The airport had growing pains and the food services struggled to maintain the pace. There was no such thing as late food delivery to the aircraft, besides the thirty-five dollar per minute fine. Invisible bells rung around the airfield. You'd hear one airline tell the other "Watch the caterer. He was late with my order yesterday."

When they pass you, you'd hear, "Had a bad day today eh, Lou?"

Lateness is tantamount to scraping the aircraft with your food truck. I was very relieved when the major airlines started to pick up and load their own aircraft. Besides, the cost to deliver and unload an aircraft was a losing proposition. We were not a specialist in that department. We really could not afford it and we lost on each delivery to a large aircraft. It tied up the loading staff, running back and forth with missed or last minute items required.

Managing a flight kitchen was remotely comparable to managing a large hotel that had twenty-four banquet halls, each demanding evening dinner service without delay. This was also keeping in mind that each banquet room averaged 90 to 330 people with 20% being first class guests that require a different upper class menu. Coordinating the kitchen preparations with the assembly staff to meet a time factor was a daily ordeal. Mass food production assembly demanded that all food reach the final stage (on the plate) in a fresh appealing form. Every aspect must be coordinated. For example if the salad was held up by the dessert this late arrival on the assembly belt line meant that the lettuce could become wilted. And then a complaint might be launched towards the stewardess presenting the meal to the passenger. Our timelines also had to take into account the necessity of advanced preparation to reach the aircraft half hour before loading it on-board the aircraft. Plus the preparation and assembly time in the flight kitchen added an hour or more of waiting before serving the meal on-board. The freshest meal presented to the passenger is three hours old, six hours on long flights.

The prepared meals suffered additional waiting time for the drinks and snacks to be served.

Keep in mind that a Toronto morning flight that picked up passengers in Ottawa then flew direct to Europe, had both its breakfast and lunch prepared in Toronto. There were no flight kitchen facilities in Ottawa. That was the reason there were so many complaints regarding airline food. So, as Branch Manager, I would receive dozens of letters of complaint. I replied to them, choosing from a dozen form letters, diplomatically phrased. My secretary would choose the letter that was best suitable to the complaint. We kept careful records as to what date each letter went out to insure that we were not too close of duplication and thus revealing our reply system.

As I have mentioned I had 138 people employed as flight kitchen personnel and that number grew over 150 people on long weekends and peak holiday times.

With constant bickering and competition between departments, and an inflated schedule on long holiday week ends I found it quite difficult to cover all bases at all times. I therefore had shift supervisors in all preparation departments. I instituted a daily shift report on each shift around the clock, including a separate daily journal for each of the restaurants and the Toronto Flying Club.

On each page of each journal there was a segregated blank space for midnight to 8:00 a.m. shift, the 8:00 a.m. to 4:00 p.m. shift and the 4:00 p.m. to midnight shift. At the bottom of each space read the comment: if you require more space, attach a separate sheet of paper to the journal. This was a tremendous time saver to help keep track of the duty performed by the supervisors of each shift. If there was no incident(s) to report, which was seldom, they were just to write "normal shift". If a problem arose on a shift and it was not reported, the supervisor found himself in a most embarrassing situation. I received many comments regarding our supervisors: "looking for him", "no where to be found", "taken off for the evening", "sleeps for two hours each night" and incriminating notes. I think the journal solved some of the problems and deterred the supervisor of many of the practices stated above.

Very seldom I appeared for work where there was not a problem to be solved or a fire to be put out. After three years, I had honoured my contract with CARA, my employer, and received a pleasant letter attached to additional three years contract, which I did not return.

The company was growing rapidly, with a philosophy of "if it works, don't change it". They were hiring vice-presidents and executives at head office, without any consideration to promote the branch managers, who were the backbone of the company. People with less experience were put in position to check and report on the airport branch managers. This was truly unacceptable, to say the least, for the managers in the flight kitchen in the airports across Canada.

At that same period in time I had been contemplating moving closer to the airport to cut down my travelling time. The owner of the company heard I was shopping for a home and he suggested I find a lovely home with a separate entrance to the basement's recreation room. They would finance the house but the title would be in my name.

That evening I discussed it with my wife, she replied "Why not? They have all your time now. Why not give them your soul." That statement stuck with me for several weeks. I made a realistic assessment of my situation. What were my future prospects? My final decision was influenced by my wife's comment but also by the actions of another man. During the same period of time, a very efficient, shrewd, hardworking manager of the Montreal flight kitchen had terminated his services. He was as disheartened by head office's promotional methods. Perhaps this also influenced me.

A year later, on just the second position I applied for, I was hired by the Toronto Board of Education to administer the high school cafeterias and create a food services department and cafeteria in the new Education Centre building located at 155 College St. near University Avenue.

I recall when my future boss D. Mewhort phoned me at work saying that the Board last night had approved me, "The job is yours!" at that precise moment my present boss was standing in front of me in the office. I simply responded to Mr. Mewhort with, "Can I call you back on this matter?"

The job was subject to the Board's Doctors mental and physical approval and I had much doubt that I would pass the physical examination. When applying for the position, I walked confidently and straight in for my interview with the Board of Education, carefully concealing my leg brace with a matching sock. I passed without notice, but this was not going to be an easy hurdle. All my scars and physical deformities had to be revealed to the medical officer. I walked out of the office of flight kitchen and didn't mention to the office manager that I had a medical appointment. I felt strange. I was looking for a way to abandon my staff who for the most part liked me although I'm sure some feared me. I was experiencing mixed feelings.

During the doctor's physical, when he was viewing my right drop foot supporting my withered leg and the numerous scares on my body, I said, "It is all up to you, Doctor, if I succeed in landing this position with the Board of Education."

I was very fortunate. The doctor had a favourite uncle who had suffered from war service.

He replied, "I am not going to hold you back! All the Board of Education wants revealed is if you are mentally fit, and that you do not have some quirk, because you will be around children, and talking to you I am satisfied you are fit."

Returning to the airport late that same afternoon, I was inundated with trials and tribulations. At that moment my mind directed me to a personal decision I must make. Stay or resign? That evening, I discussed terminating my position with CARA Corp. with Pearl. She concluded our long conversation with this statement, "If you don't take this job, don't worry. I will come to your funeral!"

A week or so later I wrote my letter of resignation, and handed it to my office manager for typing saying this is private and confidential.

Shortly after, she walked into my office, looking shocked and in a low voice said, "Mr. Trenton, are you leaving us?"

I was surprised and so touched by her simple question. During my five years as her boss I gave her so much pressure and she never complained, she just applied herself to the task.

Below I have quoted a segment from the letter of resignation that was mailed directly to the owner and president of the company:

"Dear Mr. P.J. Phalen:

I respectfully request to be released from my responsibilities as Branch Manager at the Malton International Airport in order to accept a position which I think might enhance my future endeavours."

I thanked him for the experience that I gained while I was employed with his fine company, etc. I deliberately didn't mention where I was going. I gave him six weeks notice and suggested I train one of the supervisors to replace me.

His response? Not a word. All our multiple weekly phone calls ceased. He would not talk to me directly. He sent out an executive to discretely find out where I was going.

The last week of my employment, I received a glowing recommendation from P.J. Phalen to the Board of Education with a copy mailed to my house.

Two years later I came face to face with Paul (P.J.) Phalen at a formal banquet in honour of the King of Greece, put on by the Greek Community. Mr. Phalen was hosting the King at his house as they were both sailing in a competition on Lake Ontario. We greeted each other warmly. I introduced him to my wife. He remembered the time when she shooed him off when he attempted to sweep the floor in front of a newsstand at the airport.

That same evening when we were leaving the banquet hall of the Granite Club there was a mass of Greek people with placards walking in a circle in front of the premises. The signs read "STOP PLAYING AND GO HOME AND LOOK AFTER YOUR COUNTRY".

It was a most unusual sight; the black-tie Greeks pouring outdoors and onto the sidewalk, greeting and shaking hands with their relatives and friends carrying the placards. My wife, in her evening dress, spotted her father and uncle and went to greet and hug them. They talked over the din of the crowd. At the same moment, the King of Greece was covertly guided out of the back door and into PJ Phelan's automobile.

My last six weeks at the airport were drawing to a close. I delayed publishing my departure to all my airline business associates until the last day (late afternoon to be precise). Why? I don't know. The only people I told were my buddy, the Mountie, and the doctor who checked all my employees annually. He called me for some signature or something I said happened to say goodbye.

The day arrived for my departure. It was timed deliberately for 4:00 p.m.; when both the day shift and the night shift meet. One of the supervisors gave a pleasant short speech in the crowded flight kitchen, with some people present from the restaurants. The staff presented me with a briefcase and monogrammed ivory stand with a pen in the centre. My reply to them was very brief and emotional. I then proceeded to make the rounds of the offices of the airline managers to say my good byes. I was grateful most of them had left for home.

On my way home I had so many mixed feelings. It was a Tuesday and I commenced my new position on Thursday of the same week.

Chapter 43

THE TORONTO BOARD OF EDUCATION

The year was 1963. My new employer was The Toronto Board of Education and henceforth I shall refer to it as, The Board. The Board was located at 155 College Street, west of University Avenue. At that period of time the Board was in the process of moving from the old building to the new premises referred to as "The Education Centre". The old Board building was physically moved back to make room for the construction of the new headquarters of The Toronto Board of Education.

Two days after leaving the airport, I reported to The Board of Education and my new Boss Mr. Dan Mewhort, who was head of Auxiliary Services and second in command to the Director of Education. He had a great desire to become the number one man of the board of education. Dan Mewhort was a public school teacher who worked himself up to second in command.

Our office desks were stuck together facing each other, with his secretary's desk in the other end of this large room. Everything in the old Board was in a state of flux and ready to move to the new building on the word of the contractor.

I was given a set of blue prints for half of the sixth floor of the new Education Centre in order to familiarize with the area. It was my job to establish a cafeteria to accommodate the head office personnel and anyone wishing to use the facilities, either the visiting public or staff and students from the University of Toronto campus across the street.

I spent the next few months setting down on paper the cafeteria dining room facilities and kitchen, ordering equipment, contacting wholesale food suppliers etc in order to be ready to move into the new premises.

I was allotted a generous budget, with more if need be, to accomplish this task. I proceeded to come below my allotted budget, in order to indicate to The Board of Education that they had picked the right man.

I was to find out later that the civil service sector does not work that way. You are supposed to fight for a bigger budget because it makes one sound efficient and hard-working.

Gosh I enjoyed having weekends off. To me it was like a week off every five days. I had time to cut and trim my grass, shovel the snow in front of my little duplex house instead of doing the bare necessities to your home. A new world had opened up to me. I discovered the true meaning of relax and live. Take the baby for a walk, not rush through the grocery shopping. I even slept in on Saturday and Sunday mornings. The work place was closed. There were NO phone calls. Being a civil servant it is an unwritten sin to discuss work on weekends.

I actually reached a point of feeling guilty, receiving the same generous salary for half of the hours of my previous employment, with many more benefits including medical coverage, an appealing retirement package, three weeks holiday and with a two-month summer slow down. From that aspect I thought I had died and gone to heaven.

Moving into the new building, with "The Education Centre" in platinum coloured lettering over the main entrance of the six story new structure, I settled in to the many nitty-gritty details of opening the cafeteria, to the approval and delight of the Board's personnel and the executive staff. This pleased me enormously.

I was frequently stopped in hallways and elevators, and had people introduce themselves, telling me who they were and the department they were in charge of. It was the first time the 500 to 600 people were brought together under one roof.

The Director of the Board summoned me to his office in the executive suite to let me know how pleased he was with the food operation and to acknowledge that I was seconded from the airport. He hoped I would be happy with my decision to join The Board. During our conversation, the director mentioned that I would find many of the Board's employees in and out of the cafeteria dressed in different forms of attire, "For your mode of dress I am suggesting you wear a white shirt with tie and a suit jacket. Just the way you are dressed presently. This is because you will be dealing, at one time or another, with all the personnel of the Board's Trustees including the public."

Through the years with the Board, I accepted the dress code suggestion as a command.

Soon after my joining we had the official opening of the new

Education Centre by Governor General George Vanier. He was an amputee and like a true soldier, with an entourage of provincial and board executives, he covered the halls and offices of all the floors of the Education Building, limping with the assistance of a cane. His faced revealed exhaustion and pain. Then he cut the ribbon on the front entrance and declared The Education Centre to be officially open. This ceremony was followed by a reception and a luncheon for the VIPs.

Three or four months had passed. It was very pleasant arriving to work in a brand new Education Centre building, with new office and food service and dining facilities. My title was Catering Administrator for the Board. I was to hire commercial caterers on a contractual basis to operate the Education Centre and the summer school cafeterias.

During the school year in our thirty-eight high school cafeterias we employed mature local people in the area with a supervisor, and three dieticians to circulate and solve any problems the arose. The menu was limited. There was lunch hour service only and thus these jobs were desirable, with a long waiting list. When any equipment was not working or required replacing, there was a "work order department." available to me for repairs or to replace the problem.

This may sound like heavy responsibility but in comparison to my last position it was a cake walk. Most of the catering activities were in the Education Centre. We supplied dinners, lunches, snacks and beverages to the many meeting rooms and departments in the Ed. Centre. For Trustees meetings plus exclusive groups such as principals and many teacher groups they simply needed to request a permit to use the Ed. Centre.

Also, each inaugural period, the Trustees would request catering in a school in their area, and invite the people aiding them with a winning campaign.

Above all, ninety percent of the days I left for home on time with most of the employees of the board. I saw this as a great novelty that I enjoyed for many years, until I was a confirmed civil servant and had fully adopted it as a lifestyle. And in case you think that no one wants the civil service life, there were fifteen applicants for my position, three from my old company CARA. I know this because my new boss handed me the file with the applicants. He didn't know what to do with it.

Life with The Board was not boring. One year, the Trustees (who are the politicians of the Board) asked for a report on how I would administer the high school cafeterias if we tendered them all out to commercial catering companies. I created a plan in three districts and tendered out a separate caterer for each group. Each bid was for two years. I felt this was a good plan since it created competition with each caterer as well as guaranteed top quality food for sale for the students.

The Trustees thought it was a great report and I received many compliments.

In actual fact (unbeknownst to me) I was hired for that specific reason; to eliminate high school cafeterias operated by the school system. The Trustees thought if all twenty-eight cafeterias could be tendered out it would save the Board a considerable amount of money.

I was advised to get ready to implement the plan commencing the September of the next school year. However, when the plan was leaked out to the news media, all hell broke loose. The cafeteria employees contacted their strong union and threatened a strike. It became a legal battle and The Board had to back off. The cafeteria employees never forgave me for my involvement. They did not realize I was also a civil servant like they were and as an employee I had to conform to The Board of Education's wishes. That commenced the discontent about the quality of the food in the cafeterias and it never subsided.

A year had passed and up came Expo 67 in Montreal. The trustees wanted to send as many students to Montreal as possible. Preparation for this undertaking actually commenced a year in advance. With meetings and sub-meetings, principals and teachers were selected to serve on committees. Coordinating such an undertaking was a big problem. The project was created by a friend of mine, Mr. Jim Peters. He was the head of the public schools Social Studies department and our offices were located on the same floor.

We discussed the feasibility of it daily. We concluded if we didn't involve the Trustees of the Board this project wouldn't fly. We had to follow protocol. Our superiors had to be informed and therefore a detailed report was submitted. Trustee W. Ross adopted the plan as his own brain child. He declared himself chairman of the project. This was an advantage for us because it became easier to process and get passed for approval by the Board. It was, in fact, passed with full approval by the Board as they said "It is all systems go!"

Every elementary and middle school Principal and teacher was involved in the Expo 67 Project by arranging transpiration, choosing students and parents for escort duty and basic coordination and administration.

My part was also challenging. I had to arrange for a three-day period: milk midway to Montreal, then breakfast and lunch at the Expo grounds and a dinner on the premises where we had the students billeted; with a variety of menus for each day. It was a three-day cycle, repeated weekly, for eighteen hundred students. It was a great adventure for them and a big responsibility for the Board to undertake.

We went over the estimated budget and the chairman of The Board, also the chairman of the project, was being criticized for going over budget on the matter. In desperation the chairman called me at home, demanding I down-grade the food arrangements on the menu my committee had approved. He suggested we substitute the bacon and eggs for breakfast with Corn flakes in an individual box portion plus a half pint of milk. I immediately refused this and the other suggestions he demanded. I replied, "Sir, you are representing the biggest school board in the country. You will get much criticism from the parents who are paying for their children to attend on this trip. You represent a Ward where all the students are attending this trip for free because they are less fortunate section of the city. But, I'll submit this to the Committee as your recommendation, not mine!"

He retorted, "If you're not going to take orders, Trenton, you might as well get off this project!"

"If you wish to remove me off this project then fine", I replied. "Tomorrow I'll submit my resignation to the Director of Education, sir."

He hung up on me.

I presented the chairman's suggestions to the food committee, and they were turned down by the Expo committee. The incident was forgotten by the Chairman and I.

Expo 67 was launched with an elaborate reception in the Education Centre by the Trustees for city officials.

It is interesting to note, all the trustees made a brief visit to Montreal Expo 67 to inspect the student's food and accommodations. They flew to Montreal at The Board's expense, rented large automobiles, stayed in the best hotel rooms and enjoyed their visit to Expo 67. Yet the Trustee and Chairman of Expo 67 Project wished to economize on the children with a corn flakes breakfast, while he resided in a palatial home for a period of two months, flying back and forth between Montreal and Toronto, with a chauffeur at his disposal.

It had taken a seven-week period to process all the students on a their three-day trips to Expo 67, managed mainly by Board personnel who were uprooted from Toronto to live in Montreal for six-week period. These staff did not live in those palatial surroundings and often found themselves working odd hours of the day and night.

When the Expo staff returned to Toronto, there were a lot of ill feelings. There had been promises of promotions etc. by the Trustees that went unfulfilled. The bitterness lingered on for many years with some staff never overcoming it. As for myself, I fulfilled my responsibility (to my own and The Board's satisfaction) and expected nothing and received the same.

The Board continued with normal business. The Education Centre was always active, with a variety of meetings averaging twelve to twenty scheduled daily plus the twice monthly evening trustee meeting, with four weekly committee meetings all requiring beverage, snacks, lunches or dinners. It was business as usual.

It was most often business as usual but I should mention an interesting project that presented itself the year I joined the Board. It was spurred on by the Cuban Missile Crisis. A committee was formed by the director on demand from the Trustees of the Board. The question was asked "How would The Board handle a gas or chemical fallout in the Schools?" They gave us two months to submit a report on the situation. The Committee discussed the overall plan, and we all retired to submit a report on our particular expertise. I felt I was left with the bulk of it:

I submitted a five-page report.

In case of chemical fallout:

[a] The teachers in each class will close all windows and draw the shades.

[b] The teachers should immediately escort the children in the basement, making sure the windows are sealed.

[c] The first duty of a caretaker is to shut off the water inflow.

[d] The caretakers will lock and seal all doors, and stand guard. They are to let no one in or out of school.

For advanced preparation I further recommended:

All schools to install 500 gallon tanks for elementary schools and 1,000 gallon tanks for high schools to be connected to the water system, to be used for food preparation and drinking only. Dry food was to be purchased and stored in a dry area, enough to feed an individual school's population for a 48-hour period. Also there should be a detailed preparation guide, including portion control that the teachers needed to follow.

I suggested we test the plan with 100 volunteers over a long weekend, to reveal any oversight.

I was complimented on my report and was quite happy that we did not have to experience the real thing.

Approximately eighteen months later, the possibility of a fall out (chemical war fare) subsided. People ceased storing food in their basements, and stopped building fall out shelters in yards.

The second year of service with the Board, I was seconded into membership in the Board of Education Veterans Association, and have remained a member to this present date. The organization originated with the First World War veterans. Its main purpose was to muster up a representation for the City Hall Annual November 11th Remembrance Day Service. I reluctantly served in every office with the Veterans Association. And to this day I am stuck with the Marshall's duty each November 11th at the head of parade. I have continuously participated in the parade for the past 40 years.

The year of my presidency, I was instrumental in politicking for a Veterans subsidized pension for non-teaching staff, to be financed by the Veteran with his severance pay. This was to aide Veterans from the First and Second World Wars who were retiring; a little plan to help them keep up with the inflationary tread of the time. It required three years, with many committee meetings, to hammer out the details and then be processed through The Board to declare it law. I derived a lot of satisfaction from the successful result of the Veterans Association additional pension aide project. It now conforms to all the Veteran Teachers extra pension for service in the military.

Former location of the Education Centre, 155 College Street & University Avenue, Toronto.

Chapter 44

ENTERING THE RENTAL REAL ESTATE INVESTMENT BUSINESS

The time off on weekends gave me time to contemplate my financial future and the need for some additional security for my young family. I now had a little girl and a baby boy that would require nurturing and a university education. Rolling these thoughts in my head for some time now I thought about what I could do.

The duplex apartment I had my family comfortably housed in seemed easy for me to financially carry, with rent from the upstairs apartment unit plus the steady twice a month salary. I found my situation quite acceptable and enjoyable summer holidays caused no financial strain.

Still I felt unfulfilled. For some reason I needed additional security.

I had always enjoyed reading although I was never a reader of fiction. I favoured history, self-improvement literature plus also business books of any kind. One day a book caught my eye. The title was HOW I TURNED A THOUSAND DOLLARS INTO A MILLION IN REAL ESTATE by Mr. William Nickerson. Being very sceptical of "get rich quick" schemes, I thumbed through it. The title had aroused my curiosity but it was just over a hundred pages and, perusing the first few pages, I found it dull reading. But as I continued to read I found it was quite down to earth reading material, and it made a lot of sense. The first couple pages which covered a step-by-step start were quite clear to me. I was already into rental real estate in a humble way.

I purchased the soft cover book, and for the next while commenced devouring every detail. I quickly reached a degree of great desire to swim into the real estate waters with both eyes closed. I cannot remember how I managed the down payment. It was probably part savings, part borrowed from the bank. I purchased my first investment, a fourplex on Northcliff Avenue in Toronto by applying Mr. Nickerson's book as a guide and advisor. In fact (although I didn't know it at the time) I used this book as a crutch to lean on.

The four unit apartment building was fully rented and I based my decision to purchase on whether or not the investment would carry itself; mortgage payments, interest and capital, taxes, plus heating costs in winter. Any unusual, unforeseen expenses such as a roof leaking, furnace break down, plumbing would come out of my salary. Snow removal was my responsibility. I carried a snow shovel in the trunk of my automobile.

I would not invest in a rental income property if the revenue did not equal the mortgage interest payments adding an equal amount to enhancing the capital in the building. Simple arithmetic revealed the answer.

Real estate investment was and is a long term proposition. You will loose if you decide to sell after just a couple of years. The legal fees and the real estate commission plus trivia closing adjustments will consume all profit if any is to be had. If you can't afford to tie up your money for five, preferably ten years, find some other investment.

Completing the sale, taking ownership and management of the building, I found myself deep in debt yet somehow a feeling of stability rose over me. Or was it the pride of ownership? The rental situation went well, without any major problems. Two or so years later, after much shopping and investigating with my pencil a pad, mentally swaying back and forth, should I or should I not? I finally purchased the second fourplex on 1135 Avenue Road around the corner from my duplex and residence.

What drew me to this fourplex apartment building was it was undervalued and it was in a good location near transportation and schools. Its price tag was puzzling. I checked with the city work order and they replied that the property was clear of any violations or work demands.

Submitting an offer to purchase revealed that three people owned and had recently purchased the building, just eighteen months previously. They were friends who had reached a state of disagreement and stopped communicating. They decided to withdraw their investments and break up the partnership and friendship. They had stopped socializing and now just wanted their funds out of it.

It was placed on the market and was listed by accident some thousands of dollars below what they paid for the property.

A day or two before closing the sale I received a call, to cancel my firm signed offer. They had changed their minds. I replied, "I have my bank and mortgage commitment in place. It would be a costly situation for me to oblige you". The sale was completed.

The time and effort spent managing and administering the above properties was minimal.

I designed and had mimeographed my own application forms for incoming tenants to complete and sign with receipts for the first month and a security deposit which would credit him for the last month of the lease. I also designed and printed a reminder note for rent past due, that was ready for my signature, which I mailed on the fifth day past due.

Some people are career trained. I do not consider myself expert on anything. I used the method of "necessity is the mother of invention". If I am passionate about a project I analyse and reason out the investment..

Of course some problems will arise when owning property. Some problems that I, as an apartment owner, dealt with, were:

I had a furnace that had been converted from coal to oil. One mild winter day a tenant phoned complaining the furnace would not start. To save an expensive service call I snuck out of the office to try to start it. Attempting to start the furnace I flooded it. When it ignited the flame proceeded to climb to the top of the low ceiling. I yelled to the tenant, who just arriving to see what the problem was, to have her call the fire department! By the time the fire engines arrived, the excess oil burned off, the flame subsided on its own and I got the furnace operating.

Another winter it snowed all weekend long. Monday I went to work but forgot to shovel the snow. The tenants complained about the snow not being removed from the sidewalk. They called the city authorities and they tracked me down at The Board. (My employer.)

On one occasion, I was late submitting a payment on an oil invoice. They phoned my place of work. I was not available so the girl on the switchboard directed the call to my superior. My boss located me and said, "These people sound mad. Take time off and settle the account." Which I did that day, and terminated their service.

Experience taught me not to become too familiar with tenants.

They would demand from the owner a new paint job because they felt their apartment looked grubby. Or they'd ask for a new stove because the old stove was scratched. Or the refrigerator was not cold enough or the floor needed maintenance or any other number of complaints. I found it best to answer questions by mail and sound official and formal at all times. Most people disliked replying through the post office as it was too inconvenient.

The renting situation was at a premium in those days and there was much concern over vacancies with the mortgage and taxes that had to be paid. When a vacancy occurred, my wife and I would double check the vacant apartment, clean up any extras then advertise it. My wife would book appointments for evenings Monday to Fridays, and mornings and afternoons on the weekends. I would go and greet the potential tenant, exhibit the empty apartment, always hoping and ready to sign him up.

I didn't say the rental business was easy business to be in. It was just easier compared to operating your own restaurant.

Approximately five years later, I turned those three little apartment buildings into one 44 suite apartment building. Working at my regular position with The Board, I came to conclusion if I streamlined a bit I could take over a larger apartment building. I could hire a superintendent to look after the maintenance of it. That would render me some relief from shovelling show in the winter and mowing grass in the summer and would advance my progress in the rental business and boost my pride and morale a little.

Selling the three small buildings rendered me enough funds to purchase a private home for my family. This was my first domicile with a private front lawn and yard for my offspring.

Finalizing the purchase and taking possession of the forty-four suite apartment, four story complex at 2960 Keele Street in North York, filled me with much pride for the progress I had made. It was new, (just three years old!) with an impressive, white-glazed brick surrounding the exterior. This was one of the desirable points when purchasing it. I named it ATHENIAN COURT Apartments. The apartment name was influenced by a family holiday on the Mediterranean with a bus tour of the city of Athens and a stop-over to my place of birth in northern Greece.

I received notoriety in the Real Estate Brokers Monthly circular talking about how I turned three small retail units into one modern 44-unit apartment complex, with pictures emphasizing, in colour, the larger building and dynamic looks. The article ended with "We can do the same for you! Call us!" I was pleased I gained familiarity renting smaller apartment buildings.

1135 A and 1135 B on Avenue Road, Toronto

147 Northcliffe Boulevard, Toronto

191 Castlefield Avenue, Toronto

Athenian Court Apartments 44 Suites
2960 Keele Street Metro Toronto Rental properties
owned and operated by me as a side line for over 25 years.

Chapter 45

MANAGING A LARGER APARTMENT BUILDING

Operating and administrating a larger building places you in a different category. I needed to adapt to the change. Instead of less, it was a little more time consuming. At the offset, I informed all tenants by mail, to submit monthly rent by cheque to the apartment superintendent and a receipt would be issued to them. I also supplied the superintendent with application forms for rent and printed notices for rent due.

When a vacancy came up it was best, each time, to remind the superintendent to place the sign on the front lawn advertising it and that he should be available to show and rent the unit to responsible people.

It was my practice to drive-by to check that the vacancy sign was displayed on the lawn. I emphasized this to the superintendent that if we missed a month of revenue, it was not retrievable. But really why does the superintendent care? He gets his free apartment plus a few hundred dollars monthly for his services!

I refurbished the nice lobby in the main entrance with furniture and paintings. The front of the lobby was a glass wall, overlooking the cemented veranda with guard rail on each side. I installed a huge cement bowl filled with flowers to give the place an attractive, classy, homey look. On the lawn I planted eight, fast-growing mountain ash trees for privacy and shade from the morning sun. Surrounding the front lawn in a U shape touching one end of the building to the other, I installed a drooping, white, chain link fence to match the same colour bricks on the building.

I was quite pleased with the bit of renovation. Then I realized what kind of people some tenants are. The superintendent related some of his observations to me. The flowers planted in the cement cauldrons were going missing. Some adult tenants, when entering the apartment, would pick a bunch of pretty flowers to place on their dining room table to grace their evening meal. One tenant, dressed for work, supplied his morning boutonniere from those flowers. The tenant's attitude was "Why not? I pay my rent!"

The lobby furniture and the pictures hanging on the wall found their way into the tenant's apartments. When they moved, the pictures they borrowed from the lobby became their property.

One tenant who moved out of his apartment, left it in immaculate condition so we returned his security deposit in full. However, when the new tenant moved in we discovered the refrigerator motor was missing. And there was an area blackout, due to hydro failure, and some tenants wanted to move to a hotel at the landlord's expense.

One morning a tenant could not manoeuvre his automobile up the wet ramp of the underground garage. He stayed home and demanded a day's pay from the landlord.

In addition to those tenant issues there was the apartment unit that was located above the furnace room. On very quiet days you could hear the furnace working away. The nervous new tenants turned ballistic, fearing that if the furnace developed a problem it would blow up and they would be killed. They pleaded to be moved away from the furnace room.

On several occasions automobiles were left abandoned in our parking lot. I would phone the police but the sergeant at the station was often reluctant about having to remove the automobile with a police tow truck. On those occasions it would be picked up by a private tow company, within the hour. No receipt would be left with the superintendent as to where the car was going, or where the auto could be retrieved.

I soon became aware that there was a different class of tenants residing in smaller building units versus the larger ones.

During my fifth year of apartment operation, it was time to evaluate my situation. Was I going to quite my job with The Board and go into this business full-time? I have been contemplating veering off to drive on this road for some period of time now. However, arranging finances to purchase a larger (over 100 unit) apartment building along with maintaining my present building would not leave me with the revenue necessary to hire a professional management company to relieve me of the administration and travelling which consumed much of my time. Undecided, I invited one of these professional real estate management companies to meet with me for lunch.

I stated my intent and he made his pitch which was convincing and appealing to me. I said I would let him know and he left some literature for me to convince me they were the best in the business.

A month later the same company name was headline news being accused of absconding with thousands of dollars in rent revenue from a client. Interestingly this expose did nothing to encourage nor discourage me to forge ahead and proceed with this project. I have not yet clarified it to this day.

Chapter 46

NEGOTIATING, FOR SALE

I placed a small ad in the appropriate section on the Toronto Star offering my beautiful Keele St. building up for sale. I received six or seven inquires and all petered out except one. He kept phoning and asking details. In fact, he inspected the building on two occasions. He made a verbal offer of $75,000 down payment less then my asking price. I turned it down. He replied, "Okay I get my real estate agent to call you."

I replied, "That is fine but you will pay his commission, over and above my asking price." I said.

Negotiations stopped for three or four months. Then he finally, (through his lawyer) submitted a written offer, to my surprise, for twenty-five thousand above my fixed price. His offer was subject to me agreeing to accept part of the down payment as a mortgage he possessed on the residential home. Much to his delight, I agreed. We finalized and closed the deal. It was a win-win situation. I accepted a $150,000 second mortgage plus a second mortgage of $8,500 on his house, per our agreement. I also agreed to receive a lower monthly payment, for an extra two percent above the 5 percent current rate of mortgages in that period of time, for a total of seven percent. The above transaction, automatically introduced me to the mortgage business.

It was a reverse process since I was so accustomed to paying mortgages. This was a magical, pleasant interlude with this change of business affairs. I had extra cash flow, extra time and I was easily able to maintain my position with the Board. I'll discuss this further. I could not have managed the time to enter the real estate rental market and hold down a position with CARA Corp. at the International Airport.

Two or three years later I received a notice from the purchaser's lawyer asking me to repair the cracking and disintegrating white glass bricks on the building as it was suggested by the city building inspectors. At considerable legal cost to both sides, I prepared to enter the court room for a legal settlement.

On discovery it was pointed out by my wife Pearl, that the building inspectors report read "should be repaired" and NOT a demand to repair the glazed bricks on the exterior of the building. This oversight by both lawyers revealed resulted in a no contest case and a savings of $75,000 for me.

As I mentioned above, at this stage in my life I was 51 years-old, my home was free of mortgages. I had attained a new plateau.

I should mention that the only downside to my selling the apartment building was felt by my loving daughter Becky. She was disappointed I sold it because I had promised her an apartment to study in if she continued her education at York University which was close by. My son, Mark, a happy-go-lucky kid, dear to my heart, felt this less as he was just entering high school.

Front of the Trenton Inn in Antartikon, Greece. I am on the left, next to me is cousin Tonas, then Percephone and Paskaleni Trenton, October 1993.

A picture of Trenton taking a picture of a Trenton (my grandfather) which was hanging in the Inn at Antartikon, October 1993.

Travelling with friends. From left: Julie Peters, I, Percy, Jim Peters. Taken on our fourth trip to the village of Zhelevo to gather information for my family tree.

I and my wife, with two friends (front of us) hopping in the Caribbean Islands.

Shore leave, on a Greek Island, mxv Jupiter, 1985.

I and my wife, November 1996. We are not cottage people, we managed one or two trips per year.

Chapter 47

THE MORTGAGE VENTURE

With the excess funds at my disposal and already holding two mortgages, I had dipped my finger in to test the "mortgage" waters. I cemented my familiarization with this game by reading as much literature on the subject as I could. It felt odd now being on the receiving side of the mortgage game.

A month after beginning my research, I received my first on-the-job experience. Mr. Demello, the owner of my Keele Street building wanted to pay off his $8,500 mortgage. I went to his house located in the west-end of the city on a street. His row home was attached to a strip of eight homes. I received a cheque for the outstanding amount and I presented them with a receipt. I suggested that they contact their lawyer and he could send me letter for my signature. I had to repeat myself as they were of Portuguese-speaking with English as a definite second language. Then I left with my cheque, ready to be reinvested. It was that easy. This transaction [my first] terminates all debt from the borrower, referred to as the Mortgagor. I was the Mortgagee. A month or so later I received from his lawyer a release document for my signature which basically confirmed he has paid in full.

I decided to lay out a plan. The interest coming in from any mortgage would be reinvested in another mortgage unless some other attractive investment looked more appealing.

I have never made a habit of discussing the details of my personal business with friends at work or strangers, however I seized every opportunity to talk in general about the subject of mortgages and real estate. Sometimes I left associates with the impression that I dabbled in mortgages. That was as close as I got to revealing my business. I could have approached a number of people, friends and associates in the real estate business for contacts to purchasing mortgages but again, I played it low-key.

I found a specialist dealing directly in mortgages, a broker, through an ad in the newspaper section. He, being a stranger to me and I to him, made me more aware of what I was doing. I never hesitated to decline an offer to purchase if it didn't feel right. I was also aware that the broker is promoting himself as an honest man who would not deliberately steer anyone into a risky purchase. He wants to retain you as a client and befriend you. Having said that, it was always a situation of "Let the buyer beware".

Each month a mortgage broker published a list of mortgages for sale, detailing the interest rates, discount rate, number of years and a brief background on the mortgagor. From that information you choose to bid on the mortgage. Your decision had to be almost instant because the broker had a number of clients, biding at the same time. It was a "first come, first serve" game.

The mortgage broker would familiarize you with his monthly list that was mailed to you. He would also give advice to his new clients in order to gain your confidence. As I've said, my broker was an honest man but once you were familiar with the business you were left on your own to use your best judgment when choosing mortgages.

Like many investors, I did not wait to receive the monthly list through the mail. I had them call me the hour it was available. Within two hours I found myself sneaking out of work and over to his office to peruse the list. I would often decide right there whether I was going to buy or not. And another advantage of being in the broker's office was if a particular mortgage did appeal to you, they had a little more detail on file about that mortgage that would aide you in your decision.

Each monthly visit to my friendly broker added a little spice to my life along with some trepidation about deciding whether or not I should plunk down my block of thousands. Sometimes I wanted to give a mortgage a little more thought but when I returned to the office and decided to purchase the mortgage it was too late; it had been sold. Remember, I was competing with my broker's clients.

My desire for security did not permit me to terminate my amicable job with The Board of Education. Mortgages were my exciting, profitable sideline so for the next fourteen years, until I reached retirement age, I quietly and undramatically reinvested all interest earned, including mortgage payoffs. I created my own record system, which permitted me easier and a more understandable control of my investments. One can purchase a system that is designed for mortgage control but having perused them, I found my method of record keeping was clearer to me.

It was not all smooth sailing. Late monthly payments were normal with some clients, but a standard printed monthly reminder most of the time solved that oversight. Overall, I found that losses added up to approximately five percent of my total investment.

To prevent one loss I went knocking on the mortgagee's door to try and collect payment that had not come for three months. When I asked him for the payment, he simply handed me the keys to the house. I did not accept the keys as I would be violating city by-law by throwing a man out on the street like that. A judge would reprimand you and you could receive bad publicity, if the media heard of it. They loved stories of that nature. So I contacted my lawyer and prepared the necessary documents and handed them over to a bailiff. Unfortunately there were so many new immigrants from India residing in the premises with the same or similar name it was impossible to serve the person responsible for the mortgage. Under such circumstances, the only thing left to do is to bide your time. When he tries to sell the house he would require the mortgagees (my) signature for a clear title, to permit future sale of the premises. And that was the most serious mortgage problem I encountered. The rest were just slow payment reminders, leading to phone calls and legal threats with very few follow-throughs.

Hey, I didn't say it was easy business, but the profit is certainly there. I know of no business free of trials and tribulations.

While creating, planning, and putting many bank loans in place to permit me to operate and administer an income real estate operation I needed to maintain my managerial civil service position, for two reasons:

1. The salary was necessary to support my family.

2. The stability of the job rendered it easier to obtain all my short and long term loans (which is the life-line of real estate manoeuvring).

Entering the mortgage investment market relieved me of the necessary monthly visits to the apartment building and increased my working capital required for my new challenge in mortgage investments. Besides, it was a welcome relief to spend time with my family, and have a little more time for travelling.

Chapter 48

THE PLEASURES OF TRAVELLING

Almost every winter the family and I were off to Florida for a holiday. With much pre-planning and excitement, each Christmas we would pack our summer clothing and other paraphernalia and stuff the trunk of our car with not an inch to spare. I would say a silent prayer for our aging automobile to be able to transport us to our destination and back home safely. We always departed very early in the morning. Many times we had to shovel the deep snow in the driveway to gain access to our car. My young son, Mark, would remark as we shovelled the deep snow, "Hope Mom don't change her mind."

Loading the trunk of that car served as traction through the unplowed city streets. It was fine once we were on the 401 highway heading for the US border. It was an adventure driving eighteen hundred miles two and a half days on the road. The first day we cleared the snowbelt. The second day we were into spring weather. Shedding some of our winter clothing at that stop at the motel we would change into short sleeves and prepare for the summer climate for the next two weeks.

The night before departing for the sojourns it was almost mandatory to visit my children's Grandmother (Baba) Sophia. She would wish us bon voyage and pack a lunch for the four of us that would last us all the way to Florida. We'd have picnics at the rest stops on the long scenic journey. The family looked forward to that trip south each and every year.

On only two occasions did we experience car problems. Once was in the thick of the city of Atlanta, Georgia when in all the stop and go traffic our car over-heated. It was a Russian car I had purchased at The Auto Show, brand new, for the sum of $3,700 including taxes. It was sturdy as a tank but the mechanical aspect required improving. The car would not re-start and we were on the outside lane of an eight-lane highway in the middle the city. Luckily with the assistance of a kind motorist we managed to push the car off to the side, clearing the driving lane. We had to wait until the engine cooled down for twenty or so minutes but then we were on our merry way.

The other auto occurrence was a shimmy in the front. We pulled into a highway service station and got it adjusted and we were on our way down the highway, without purchasing the four tires they recommended.

One time on a trip to Florida my son Mark, who had just recently got his driver's license, moaned and begged me to let him drive. It was the first new car I had ever purchased but it was a straight highway so I gave him the wheel. However it was his first time on the highway and I guess me letting him drive gave him too much confidence. We were stopped by the highway patrol in Kentucky. The fine was $125 – on the spot! I sympathized with him, but Mark's mother insisted on him paying the speeding ticket to teach him a lesson. So said his mother! However, if I had not secretly subsidized his loss, he would have had unhappy holiday in Florida.

Some years we drove down to Florida in convoy with friends, and their children who were the same age as our own children. Driving seamed to be a convenient way to motivate around with a family. I found it also rendered temporarily relief from pressures of business. And can add a bit of humour. The first two hours on the highway of a lengthy holiday we had planned from Toronto to BC, my very young son said to me, "Dad when do we get to Vancouver? Because I want to go back home to play with my friend Bruce."

That summer we motor toured west all the way to Vancouver Island then we turned south boarding a ferry to the state of Washington. We decided to drive home via the United States, heading south as far as California's beautiful Pacific Coast line to San Francisco. We then drove east, with a stopover in Las Vegas, Nevada (where children were not permitted in the casinos) and on into Colorado. We then headed north, up and into the state of Illinois via Chicago and then crossed the border at Sarnia to our beautiful Canada.

The following summer we drove to the east coast city of Halifax, and then took the ferry to Newfoundland. It was a great experience for the kids. I thought that when they studied geography in school they could say, "I've been there."

The rest of the summer was spent with having day trips on the weekends to Wasaga Beach for a swim with family and friends.

However they were not as numerous as I would have liked them to be. Wasaga Beach was of course my old stomping ground and I liked the nostalgic feel.

We also had numerous trips to Europe, with and without the children. One trip we flew to Scotland and rented an automobile. I drove to the many places to show my wife where I was stationed in war time. Then we crossed over to France and toured the areas of Normandy where I landed on the invasion. It was a very emotional experience like a bad dream that happened to someone I knew. It was too strange and remote to have happened to me. Two days later we drove out of France and into Germany. I drove on the famous Autobahn Highway at 2.00 A.M. because we could not find a place to stay for the night. So with no choice we kept driving with short rest periods in the car.

The next day we crossed into Austria and then attempted to enter Czechoslovakia, without success. We drove south to Yugoslavia and toured around for a day or so. Then we headed for Greece by approaching the Macedonian border. We had little problem at the border because we were asked, "If you were born in Greece, why can't you speak Greek?" Questions like these do delay your entry and show who has the ultimate authority. (Which was a big issue for all Macedonian-speaking, Greek-born immigrants.)

From the border we drove to ancient and world re-known city of Athens to attend a convention. I was there to represent the Toronto Chapter (called the Lord Byron Chapter C.J.1) of The American Hellenic Educational Progressive Association, of which I was president that year. It was a five-day stay in Athens. We met up with my favourite cousin Helen and her husband Gus Marmon, who were surprised to see us. Gus hadn't given us much hope driving from Scotland to Athens to be in time for the convention. We successfully met our schedule.

We attended all the necessary meetings and social events including one formal affair. It was held beachside with an orchestra playing. All night long one could hear frequent long zaps of the mosquitoes committing suicide by flying into a blue attractive light fixture posted around the dance area of this classy hotel complex.

The convention came to a close and we headed north again to my humble village concealed in the mountains of Macedonia. I often wondered should I have resided in my place of birth and what type of a person would I have been? Certainly not what I am now. What effect did the war years have on me? If I had stayed would I have survived the war? I was definitely a different human being, that's for sure. I would not be speaking English. I would have been fluent in Greek, speaking in two languages and writing in one. I would most likely be a farmer married and eking out a living by the sweat of my back. I wondered a lot as I entered the village again.

On four occasions, we visited our childhood village (Pearl was also from Zhelevo).This specific visit we spent two days re-introducing ourselves to the very few relatives left in a ghost town. This was unfortunately the status of most of the villages we drove through our lovely Macedonia.

Next morning it was time to say adios, with farewell hugs and God bless to all. We drove heading southeast to the little city of Yannina. My father had done his Army training here when he was inducted to serve in the Greek army. I do not know why that thought came in to mind at that particular time it made me feel closer to my father.

We checked into a hotel in the centre of the city and that evening after supper we walked (in Greek, they call it a "volta") the main streets of the town and picked up some unique souvenirs that were made right before your eyes. Watching the man practice his art by creating our souvenir and emblem of the Macedonian sun burst made the purchase memorable and special.

The next morning we always rose early. Within an hour or so we reached the Port of Igoumenitsa just in time to drive our rented English car onto the ferry ship heading for the island of Kerkira, on the Ionia Sea. We spent the night on the island and attended the elaborate casino. The next morning we were back on the ferry heading for the shore of Brindisi on the tip of Italy. We got off the ferry and onto the main highway heading for Rome where we toured that city plus the great Vatican.

On the second day we left Rome in the early morning. Their modern main highway went through and not over the mountains. Some of the tunnels were a kilometre long and well-lit. Their highway gasoline stations like Esso had a four or five-story hotel facing the gas pumps. Even here the food was incredible. Without a doubt, the best prepared and tastiest food in all of Europe exists in Italy.

Reaching the Swiss border, we were permitted to enter the country without incident. We thought my Macedonia contained huge mountains until we saw the Switzerland's monstrosity in height and steep hills. Our auto strained and required checking water almost hourly. We spent one night on one of these mountain tops. It was very cold even under three or four blankets and this was the first week in August! On our way we stopped and made a snowball on the side of the road with the morning sun shining on us.

We had the car checked and they couldn't find any problems so we carried onto our next destination, France.

We stayed in a small hotel near the ferry dock where they lock you in at night for your own safety with an iron gate on the main entrance. I know it was because of where we were located but I joked with my wife that it was because of the drivers. We found the French drivers to be the most reckless drivers in all of Europe.

The following morning we had breakfast and checked out of the hotel. I double-checked the ferry service to England and the afternoon ferry had no reservations. It was first come, first serve. We were told to be early because it was always crowded. We had a four hour wait that afternoon. There was a line up of cars ahead of us and behind us. Time was of the essence for us because we had a long drive north to Scotland to catch a flight. We had tickets and reservations.

The ferry sails across the English Channel which is a very nasty sea. We tried to sleep with no success. Once off the ferry at Dover we commenced driving north on the main highway with one stop over. We reached The Eyers Scotland Airport with just a few hours to spare. As instructed we left the car and keys with the parking lot attendant. This was the first time I have never had a rental car thoroughly checked and a full tank of gas charged to us.

Settling down in the aircraft and flying home is always pleasant feeling. I feel sorry for vacationers who are sad to be returning to their domicile. I scheduled my time and funds to take one long family vocation and one short one annually. I found it added a balance to my life, for health sake. It helped me cope with life and its stresses.

Because of my wife Pearl's delicate health for many years we decided to take a family vacation to improve her constant physical pains. What better than a trip to Mexico at Christmas time for a little sun and fun. It was December, 2004 and my wife, dear daughter, her husband and my grandchildren (my favourite people) started off on our ideal holiday. Unfortunately, it quickly became a holiday I wish we had not embarked on. But I believe that the destination was not responsible for what occurred. The results were inevitable and could not be circumvented.

The following note was written by me on May 16th, 2005 to supply information and avoid repeating our experience to relatives, friends and for all the agencies that needed to be contacted regarding replacement lost records, my military medals, etc.

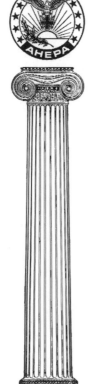

Order of Ahepa

Founded July 26, 1922

AMERICAN HELLENIC EDUCATIONAL PROGRESSIVE ASSOCIATION

C J I **Chapter Certificate**

of Meritorious Service

to

LOUIS TRENTON
PRESIDENT 1953

with grateful appreciation of the many services he has rendered to his Chapter and District, and in recognition of his unselfish contributions towards the programs and progress of the Chapter.

Presented on this 22nd day
of September ,1978.

Attest:

Chapter Secretary

Chapter President

MY FAMILY SOJOURN IN MEXICO BY LOU TRENTON

A holiday experience I do not wish on any person, friend or foe.

We planned the holiday, with joy and much excitement from the grandchildren and at considerable expense to the writer.

The day finally came when the six of us, with bags and baggage, arrived at the Toronto International Airport, at THREE in the morning, three hours in advance of our flight. After all the confusion of the baggage checking, ticket verification, X-ray processing, seat allocation, we finally boarded the aircraft. We felt totally excitement as the aircraft went racing down the runway and finally the wheels stopped rumbling and we became airborne.

The breakfast that was served on the aircraft was delicious! (I have to say so, in loyalty to my former employer CARA Corp. whom I served for five years, as the airport's branch manager of food service.) It was a very smooth enjoyable flight. Just like floating on a magic carpet. The two hour and 45 minute flight transplanted us from winter to summer.

The hotel accommodations were excellent! We were extremely comfortable, enjoying all the enmities; swimming pools for adults and children, long wide sandy beach on the Yucatan Peninsula, boating and all sorts of game activities.

The food was par excellent. It was available anywhere you walked on the vast compound of this luxurious hotel. Most impressive was the evening meal with a dozen main entrees, and two dozen dessert choices. This was no place to be if you are on a diet! The wife declined supper, a bit of jet lag she said.

The following morning my wife Persephone was not feeling any better. We summoned the hotel's physician. He administered medication, supplied prescriptions, and instructed her to spend the day in bed. The next morning, she was unable to leave her bed.

With haste we called an ambulance to transport us to a hospital 35 miles to the city of Cancun. Upon arriving, she was immediately rendered attention and mediation etc. The doctors revealed my wife had developed pneumonia.

The situation progressed down-hill thereafter. While she was going through a series of tests, and receiving medications, she had two life or death relapses. The results of the many tests revealed that immediate surgery was absolutely imperative. A team of surgeons was assembled for the operation at midnight in this very busy little hospital.

Following surgery a minimum of three weeks recuperation time was absolutely necessary.

Our holiday period had terminated. I instructed my daughter Becky to return home with her family. I would stay with my wife. I was thinking to myself, "I'll bring her home alive or in a box." My daughter perhaps read my mind and she vehemently refused to leave her mother and old dad. Therefore, she ordered her family to pack up and go home. My daughter and I stayed with our sick patient.

A week had passed. My daughter, (after a telephone conversation with her husband in Toronto), approached me in a solemn voice. She said, "Dad, I have very bad news and some very, very good news. (My dear daughter strained to break the bad news gently to me.) There was a Fire. Your home has burnt down to the brick walls. All furniture and contents are completely destroyed. The good news is you'll be getting a new house. It was insured, I hope?"

To say the least, the news was devastating.

Two weeks had passed and our sick patient was still not fit to travel on a commercial airline. We had no choice but to order an air ambulance that took another week to arrange.

Finally, two husky nurses, one male, one female, from the ambulatory aircraft, appeared at the Hospital at midnight with a stretcher and medical paraphernalia. They swooped us up and within thirty minutes from the hospital to airport we were airborne with the two nurses in a small Lear jet.

Stepping out of the aircraft in Toronto it was sub-zero weather. Being the bright guy that I am, I became aware I was wearing summer attire. The ambulance driver threw a winter parka over me. We arrived at St Michael's Hospital at 4.45 a.m. I settled my wife in bed and I was sad. I had no home to go to. The ambulance driver noticed the dilapidated appearance and condition I was in. The kind man, Mr. Fox of the Fox Ambulance Co. insisted on driving me home but I had no home to go to.

And I desperately had to keep it a secret from my wife. I bunked in my daughter's house, until my wife was ready to leave the Hospital.

Presently, we reside in a condominium apartment, and shall be, for the next three or four months or until construction to our home is completed.

This is but a very brief account of the stress and strain, my daughter and I underwent. The full details would make for very unpleasant reading.

I pass on to you the experience I gained from the above catastrophe.

1. Packing for a holiday, do not be concerned if you forget your tooth brush or shaving gear at home.

2. Packing for a holiday, do not worry if you forget to bring your favourite polo shirt, or bikini.

3. REMEMBER, DO NOT LEAVE HOME WITHOUT TRAVEL INSURANCE!

To give you an example, for the first five days of my wife's hospital stay I was handed a demand invoice for the sum of $14,300 and this DID NOT include the doctor's invoices. They were extra and forth coming.

The air ambulance to Toronto cost $108,000.

I was very fortunate the travel insurance company verification and paperwork revealed full coverage.

Also, with the insurance on our house, I was lucky enough to dot all the I's and cross all the T's that qualified us for full coverage. The cost for construction and replacement of our contents will be in excess of $385,000.

I have never been this lucky with insurance claims! In the past when I was involved in scrapes with my automobile, when inquiring about payment, The Auto Insurance Co. would say, "Better pay for it yourself, or your policy could be cancelled or future payments will increase."

Financially, the wheel of fortune spun and stopped in our favour. It could have ended in disaster. Above all, I am pleased that my wife's health is steadily improving.

An update to this note followed some three months later.

My wife, Pearl Trenton died on August 25, 2005 from excessive complications after undergoing surgery at Sunnybrook Hospital in Toronto.

And the living are left to carry on with life, whether one likes it or not, waiting for one's turn to arrive and enter into oblivion.

Most humans enter this world like all other creatures, without choice as to whose child you will be. We are raised by people we call mother and father. You have to get to know these strangers and the mother and father have to familiarize themselves with you and nurture you into adulthood.

It makes you wonder how much influence the parents have had on you or is your walk through life is pre-ordained?

It is a fact that the old remember the most minute instances of long past years.

Which reminds me, and I would be remiss if I didn't mention the following person who had maintenance over me, at a tender age, my Aunt Keta who was so much like a mother to me I feel I had the privilege of having a second mother.

My second mother, Keta Trenton, was the first person to meet me with my cousins (her children) at Union Station. When I lived with mother Keta for three years she truly adopted me as one of her own children and treated me equally.

As the years drifted by, I developed great admiration for this lady's tenacity. She had shown courage and strength to keep her family together and instil stability in her household. She worked to purchase a permanent home for her family.

On Aunt Keta's last week on earth, her daughter Sophie drove her to my house. She was so weak she was unable to get out of the automobile for a cup of tea and a visit. Unbeknownst to us, we said our goodbyes on my driveway since she was unable to come into the house. She said, "I just come to say goodbye, Louis."

She passed away that week. She was one of the first Macedonian arrivals to Canada. All her children were born in Toronto. This lady was one of the original immigrants from Macedonia struggling for survival in this new found land.

Dostori
Talos
The End

PHOTOGRAPHY

Our Wedding Day in 1954. From left standing: Philip Trenton, young Johnny Patskou, George Lazenkis, brother Laz Trenton, Fred Floras, Chris Papageorge, thebride/groom Louis&Pearl, sister Marina Marko, sister Kay Patskou, Sophie Trenton, Jennie, cousin Helen Lazenkis.

My wedding 1954 the reception (font row left) my dear father John, brother Laz, brother-in law Louis Yankou, my sister Christena Yankou, I and the bride Persephone, my mother-in law Sophia, Kay Patskou, Dona Patskou, my father-in law Vassil Patskou. (Back row) Linda and Chrissie Lou Yankou, Chris Marko, Mara, Marina Marko.

L.L. Trenton, completed advanced Infantry & Commando
training, Camp Borden, 1943.

Alexander Trenton. I am proud to say that all Trentons who were
old enough to serve in the Second World War did their duty.

Back to School after the War, with a class of veterans. I am in third row right end, Jim Piskaris is first row right end. I also attended a semester at Cornell University, USA.

Certificate for attending Summer School of Hotel Administration at Cornell University.

Seeing us off, at the Toronto International Airport. My father-in-law, Bill, with back to camera is my dear father, John, my wife and I, our dear friends Mr.&Mrs. Gus and Eileen Haba.

The War Veterans Association, of the Toronto Board of Education (TDSB) presented me with above plaque in recognition as president. And advancing the retirement pension of all employees, who served in the armed forces.

[top left] I and my wife Percy sitting on a beach.
[lower left] My wife Percy with my children Becky and Mark.
[right side] Becky and Mark on their graduation day.

The future King of England, His Royal Highness Prince Charles, a most pleasant man to chat with. He asked my wife if she was married to me during the war? She replied, NO your Majesty, I was too young, I picked him out after the war.

Reception line, from left Julie and Jim Peters, new bride Becky (nee Trenton) Norman and Jim Norman, Mona Coxson.

Standing is my precious daughter Becky Norman (1993) in front with me are my grandchildren Scott and Katie Norman

Louis Trenton with son Mark who is holding the birthday girl Katie and sitting grandmother Percy Trenton.

Louis with grandson, Scott Trenton Norman.

RIDEAU HALL

THE CHANCELLERY OF HONOURS
LA CHANCELLERIE DES DISTINCTIONS HONORIFIQUES

November 1, 2006

Dear Mr. Trenton:

I am pleased to inform you that the Government of Canada, on the advice of the Honours Policy Sub-Committee, has approved the request of the French Government to appoint you Knight of the National Order of the Legion of Honour. You may therefore accept and wear the insignia.

As per our policy, this approval was published in the Canada Gazette four months after the donor country was informed of the decision of the Committee. A copy of the Gazette is attached. The wearing sequence of this award is referred to in the "Wearing of Orders, Decorations and Medals" on our website www.gg.ca. For a hard copy of the guide, please contact Ms. Mélanie Rita at 1-800-465-6890.

May I take this opportunity to offer you my warmest congratulations.

Yours sincerely,

Emmanuelle Sajous
Chair, Honours Policy Sub-Committee

Encl.

Mr. Louis Trenton
25 Shields Avenue
Toronto, ON   M5N 2K1

ES/mr

Liberté · Égalité · Fraternité
RÉPUBLIQUE FRANÇAISE

AMBASSADE DE FRANCE
AU CANADA

L'Ambassadeur   *Ottawa, 28 November, 2005*

N°1738

Dear Mr. Trenton,

I have the pleasure to inform you that the President of the French Republic, Mr. Jacques Chirac, awarded you the Légion d'Honneur and, on his behalf, I would like to express my heartiest congratulations upon having received such an honour.

This promotion is a reward you greatly deserve for the exemplary and outstanding behaviour you demonstrated during the fierce battles of the liberation of France and Europe. By awarding you such a high distinction, France wants to glorify a great Canadian soldier who fought for freedom. This is an achievement you can be proud of.

A date could be arranged with Mr. Philippe Delacroix, Consul General of France, should you wish to be presented this decoration in Toronto.

Yours very sincerely,

Daniel JOUANNEAU

Mr. Louis Trenton
25 Shields Avenue
Toronto Ontario M5N 2K1

42, promenade Sussex, Ottawa, Ontario K1M 2C9
politique@ambafrance-ca.org

Receiving the Knighthood of the National Order of the Legion of Honor awarded by the French Government. Read the full story on the back cover of this book.

My daughter Becky and I at a military function, 2007.

I am with Mr. Philippe Delacroix, Consul General of France for Toronto and
Major Robert Bennett, The Royal Regiment of Canada.

Witnesses, French Bastille Day and Medals Presentation, 2006.

Two of my favourite people, my daughter Becky with her husband, Jim, 2007.

Katie, my lovely granddaughter, 2006.

Scott, my grandson, who thinks I am a cats meow, 2006.

LOUIS L. TRENTON 25 SHIELDS AVE. TORONTO ON M5N 2K1
416 489 3362   **CANADA**   ***lltrenton@idirect.com***

November 25,2007

MR. ERNIE SCALE
64 THIRTY-SIXTH STREET
Etobicoke   ON 8W 3L2

Greetings Conrad Ernie:

I am delighted to receive the photograph of four smiling guys, who missed the
annialation roll call sixty years ego. We had a saying in the R.R.of C. " I don't mind
serving my country I just don't want to get killed for it "

The photo shall serve as a memento of a pleasant evening, and the pleasure of
meeting people who were as scared as I was.

Thank you most kindly and with my very best wishes for a long life of reasonable
good health.

Sincerely.

Lou Trenton

French Council's residence. Ontario's recipients of Knighthood of the French
Legion of Honour, W.W.II, Ernie Scale (centre) Louis Trenton (seated).

The male Trentons are not the handsomest lot on the planet, but do we ever produce the prettiest females on earth!

The Trentons celebrate the fabulous wedding reception hosted by Mike Trenton to
honour his daughter Melissa and the groom Mr. Paul Moro.

[above] I with cousin Mike.
The Trentons all brothers and first cousins.
[below] I with cousins Philip, Alexander & Jim.

"YOU'RE INVITED"
The next meeting of the
Macedonian Coffee Clan
will take place at
Anthony's Grill & Restaurant
1090 Don Mills at Lawrence Ave
East.
Self Serve Buffet Brunch will be
available.
On Tuesday May 6, 2008,
9:50 a.m. to 11:00 a.m.
Please bring your appetite - your
wife/husband or a friend.

With pleasure hosted by
Lou Trenton

Celebrating my deceased wife Pearl Trenton date of birth May 6, 2008.

Intelligence **   ** Dignity

*
*
Honour

Our family crest of my own design. In the centre is the Macedonian sun burst – the core of the family identity. The white and blue depicting the Greek flag, the yellow section with the doted flowers and maple leaves indicates migration, Canadian ensign is for our adopted country. The ancient figured of the Male and Female looking fondly on the Macedonian sunburst indicate we are descendants of Philip and Alexander the Great. The U shaped wreath advocates for peace to mankind. Bordering the family crest is the Macedonian and Greek key symbol.

INDEX